I0829555

Growing Up With Joy

A life shaped by The Great Depression, a War,
and a Neighborhood

Joy Stothart Gaddis

JOYFUL PUBLISHING

ISBN 978-0-578-93492-1

Library of Congress Control Number 2021912567

Printed in the United States of America

Contents

Chapter 1

Child of The Depression

To Twitchell Street with Love - August 2005

I JUST CAN'T seem to get over my love affair with Twitchell Street, and the little neighborhood where I grew up, in Coushatta, my home town. I sometimes become frustrated with the prejudice, apathy, and lack of community spirit that are often evident in this little town. But I believe we survived the desperate times of the Great Depression and World War II because we pulled through all of it together, by working, caring for, and yes, loving one another.

During my lifetime I have seen many children in this little town who come out of situations of poverty, welfare, and desperate circumstances of all kinds, go on to become well-educated, productive citizens and even in some cases, acquire a certain amount of fame and fortune.

Does this come about by chance? When it happens, is it just a lucky accident? I don't think so.

When I was growing up in Coushatta, I felt the arms of this "village" around me, providing education, opportunities for leadership and service, and wonderful examples of good citizenship and caring for the needs of others. I choose to believe that my family, with the help of this "village," pointed me in the right direction and gave me opportunities to develop and use my abilities to become a productive citizen. I am grateful for the help I received and have no illusions that I "did it on my own." The schools, churches, civic organizations, and so many individuals; good people in this little town, many I knew and some I will never know played their part, just because they were good, not because I deserved it.

When I was growing up in Coushatta, I saw one bright young boy in worn, castoff clothes, face smudged from the smoke of his daddy's blacksmith shop, steered and cheered by the collective arms of this same "village" right into our nation's capitol to serve as a page in our chief lawmaking body in Washington, D.C.; a lucky accident? No, I don't think so.

When I was growing up in Coushatta, I saw the townspeople display a spirit of togetherness and community spirit that made children feel safe and cared for even during depression days and wartime, and gave the adults a sense of belonging, ownership and responsibility. Maybe the deprivation and desperation of the Depression days and the anxiety, sacrifices, and suffering brought on by World War II helped to make us a real community, living together and working together. Is all this sense of community spirit and togetherness gone? No, I don't think so. There are signs of it all around us if we open our eyes, but it is in danger of disappearing completely if we listen to the voices of hate and divisiveness around us. Perhaps it's just a sign of the times. But Twitchell Street in the 1930's and '40's—ah! That's a different matter.

I'm not sure that I could possibly explain to my children and grandchildren in a way they could understand amid the frenetic pace of this technological society, the fascination that this relic of the past still holds for me. I'm not sure I understand it myself, because it's not a rational thing. The closest I can come to an explanation is that Twitchell Street was always kind to me. It was Twitchell Street that taught me the meaning of home and family and neighborhood. The people who lived on our street were not all kin to me but they seemed almost like an extension of our family. My mother treated everyone with respect and kindness; maybe that is the key. I can say in all honesty that I never saw my mother be rude or unkind to *anyone* and she lived to be almost 92 years old.

Even the people who just had connections to Twitchell Street, like Crippled Sarah, who ironed our clothes, and Nig, who worked in the garden; the man who brought the ice and the woman who peddled eggs and vegetables; and Beulah, who worked for the Scheens; my friends' grandparents, who represented for me the grandparents I so desperately wished for and never had. I believe with all my heart that there was not one of these people who would have hesitated to step in and intervene if they saw any of us young ones doing something dangerous or just plain wrong. They cared, they were like family to me, and each one of them made my life richer, better, safer, or more comfortable in some special way.

Beginnings

The year was 1928 and my mother, Emily Brown, came to Red River Parish, a small, rural area in northwest Louisiana to teach English and French in the Methvin School after she graduated from Louisiana State Normal College in Natchitoches, Louisiana. The Methvin school was located in a farming community about 15 miles from the town of Coushatta. I don't know why my mother, who was born in Siloam Springs, Arkansas and grew up on a rice farm near Elton, Louisiana, chose to come to the northwest part of Louisiana to teach. I don't know, but I'm glad she did because that is where she met the man who would become her husband—the man who would become my dad.

How my parents met also remains a mystery to me, but I do know that my father, Bob Stothart, who was fifteen years older than my mother, worked at the L.P. Stephens & Company General Merchandise Store (also known locally as the "big store" or the "brick store"). My dad was considered by some as one of *THE* "young bachelors about town." He was a good dancer, had a keen sense of humor, and liked to have a good time. My mother was a 19-year-old beauty from down in the "Cajun Country" near Jennings, Louisiana. Apparently information like that traveled fast in a small town, even before the days of cell phones, Facebook and Twitter.

Although I don't know the details about my parents' courtship and marriage, it must have been love at first sight, because it was a very short courtship. My mother and two other young teachers were boarding with the Snead family who farmed in the Methvin community. It was probably one of these two young women who introduced them. I was told that Bob began driving out to the Snead home and chauffeuring the three young ladies to Coushatta, where they spent weekends in a small annex to the Coushatta Hotel known as the "Doll House". This must have added a little excitement to their lives, which were spent teaching youngsters five days a week out in the boondocks.

I don't know what my parents found to do on those weekends. I do know that after a few months' time they married and the Doll House became their first home.

The Coushatta Hotel was owned and operated by Daddy's first cousin, Ermine Stothart Cagle, and her husband, Steve Cagle. It was an imposing brick structure that originated as a family home built by the Leindecker

Coushatta Hotel

family and was sometimes referred to as the "Leindecker Mansion."

The few times I remember visiting the hotel during my childhood, I was awestruck by what I considered then as the "grandness" of the place. Two of those occasions were parties; one was a birthday party for my cousin, Becky Hatfield, where we children were served birthday cake and ice cream by waiters in black suits at one of the long dining tables. The other occasion was a family Christmas party where we sat around the fireplace in the living room after dinner. I also remember my parents talking about parties they attended there, perhaps during their courtship days. I could imagine the tables and chairs being pushed back to make room for dancing. My daddy always did love to dance.

A few years after my daddy's cousin "Erkie" (Ermine) Cagle died, her husband sold the hotel to some doctors, who used it for offices and hospital space. After World War II, they tore it down to make way for a much-needed new hospital building. At the age of fourteen, I was sad to see the old relic go, but glad my mother was able to buy some of the family furniture. I willingly spent some of my free time helping her scrape and sand, stain and varnish a poster bed and marble-top dresser to help furnish the "new" bedroom Alexa and I would share in the large older home our family bought on Carroll Street. It reminded me of the old hotel and happy memories I cherished of visits there during my early childhood days.

My cousin Rex Stothart, who was several years older than I, later told me that my parents, his Uncle Bob and Aunt Emily, did live in the Doll House Annex for a while after their marriage and then moved to a larger house on Holley Street near his parents, my Uncle Gray and Aunt Mamie Stothart. They probably lived there for no more than a year or two.

Child of The Depression

After my mother finished her first and only year of teaching, she and Daddy made some big changes in order to meet their financial obligations and make plans for their future. By this time, my mother was pregnant with their first child, me, and at that time in our history most school systems did not permit married women (certainly not if they were pregnant) to continue teaching. Daddy was working as a clerk at the L.P. Stephens & Co. and didn't foresee much of a future for himself there; it was a family owned and operated business and the family was large. The time seemed to be ripe for making immediate plans for the future, so he and Emily talked the situation over.

Daddy had always wanted to own his own business but he didn't have the capital to get started. My mother had a small inheritance from her parents; Daddy had no

Baby Joy

problems securing a loan to buy and begin operating a small rural general store and gasoline service station in Lake End, several miles south of Coushatta on Louisiana Highway 1. They were optimistic; the future seemed bright at that time, their plan seemed to be working. By the time I appeared on the scene on October 5, 1929, Daddy's store was off to a good start and things were going well. The financial "crash" came less than a month later. I was destined to be a child of the Great Depression.

My earliest memories are from the time we lived in Lake End. I was born in Shreveport at the old Highland Sanitarium where my Aunt Hazel, Daddy's sister, was working as an RN doing private-duty nursing. After a ten day stay in the hospital (which was standard medical procedure at the time), my parents brought me home on a cold, frosty morning to the weathered old barn of a house where they were living near Daddy's store. Our life in Lake End was quiet and uneventful at first. Perhaps I kept things livened up enough for a while to take my parents' minds off the terrible state of the economy. Some of Daddy's men friends congregated in the store during the afternoons. My mother looked after me, did a lot of reading, and visited with neighbors when she wasn't busy with housework and cooking. A young black woman came in and helped with the housework now and then.

During that time, my mother faithfully wrote updates in my baby book, titled *Little Baby's Big Days*; several pages survive to this day and I quote now from the page titled "Each Ounce of Baby is Worth More than a Pound of Gold." This is where she recorded such vital statistics as: "Weight: Birth 7 lbs; 1 month 8 lbs; 2 months 9 ½ lbs".

Another page is titled *Baby Speaks*:

'Bye-Bye' was her first word. 'Da-da' was next. Then she learned 'chickie,' 'ma-ma,' kitty' and words like that. She started walking and talking when she was ten months old.

The next page was titled *Baby's First Christmas*. Again, I quote my mother's words from the book:

On Thanksgiving Day Daddy took Baby and I to Grandpa Brown's in South Louisiana. We (Baby and I) stayed there until Christmas. On Christmas Eve I hung up Edith Joy's stocking and Santa Claus put a rattle and a little squeaking mouse in it. When we got back home we found other presents (which she lists in detail,) including a little blue teddy bear bathrobe from Daddy and Mother, a white and blue bunting from Erkie (Ermine) and Steve Cagle.

A little later when I was old enough to ride in the car with him, Daddy would sometimes take me with him to Hanna, about three miles up the road, where there was another little store and a train station. I think there was also a post office there. I don't know why he had to make these trips, but I loved to go with him because he would always buy me a Hershey bar. I made up a little song that I sang over and over on the way. I can still remember the rhythm of it: "UP a hill and DOWN a hill to GIT some choc'lit can-dy." It must have been irritating for Daddy to listen to, but I don't remember him telling me to stop it. That little chant, "UP a hill and DOWN a hill" could well have served as the theme song for my parents' lives

Emily and Joy

during what soon became a turbulent time financially for them and millions of other families here in the USA and abroad.

Meanwhile, I played in my backyard, happily unaware of the hard times that were just ahead for my parents, who were not fully aware of the devastating implications beginning to emerge and loom like storm clouds over the economic and political spectrum nationwide. For me it was a time of peace and plenty. As soon as I was old enough to sit still, my mother read to me any book she could get her hands on: fairy tales and other children's classics, Bible stories; sometimes she even read aloud parts of the novels or magazines she was reading for her own enjoyment just to keep me still and quiet. It worked even when I didn't understand the meaning. I loved the sound of the words and the sound of her voice. I went to sleep to the sound of that sweet voice, whether she sang lullabies or the popular songs of the day. Years later, I sang these same songs to my own children as I rocked them to sleep and I still remember them to this day. Some things endure.

It was a quiet time in Lake End when the unthinkable happened. One night while we were sleeping, Daddy's store was robbed. The robbers took not only money, but everything else they could take with them in one load. This was a financial blow my family could not overcome. During the 1930's, when so many people were without jobs, robberies became quite common. We survived the "crash" but the robbery was just too much. My mother's Uncle Earl, who was also her stepfather, came to our rescue by offering Daddy a job working for him on his rice farm in the southern part of the state. My mother could not understand why Daddy was reluctant to take it.

"Bob, it is so good of Uncle Earl to make us this offer," (my mother was almost pleading). Daddy could not imagine living such a different life and in such a different place from the one he had always known.

"Emily, you know I don't like that part of the state. It's almost like going to a foreign country; nothing but flat prairie land and about half the people don't even speak English. Besides, I don't know anything about rice farming," he said. "When I got home from France after the war, I declared that I couldn't think of any reason to get farther away from Red River Parish than Grappe's Bluff, or maybe Black Lake." My mother seldom challenged his decisions, especially in financial matters, but this was different.

"I can think of one reason," my mother said quietly. "You have a job waiting for you down there." She must have been feeling desperate. I'm sure the thought came to her that she might live to regret this moment, but her common sense and courage prevailed. This time it seemed to her they had very little choice. It was South Louisiana or starve.

Bob and Joy

Welcome to Twitchell Street, 1931

This story is one resurrected from memories of events my mother told me about when I was a small child. Some of the details are memories of my own from times I went with her to visit Mercille Marston, her friend and neighbor, when I was a child. I remember well the look and feel of the place and the people involved even though it's been many years, now. The main event must have happened something like this:

"Oh, Emily, come on in!" Mercille exclaimed. "It's so good to see you again after all these months. And so much has happened in our lives—good and bad—I'm still mad at Bob for taking you way off across the river over to Lake End just so he could open up a little old country store!" Both women laugh as Mercille opens the door and invites her friend Emily into her small, pleasant living room. They have missed one another.

"You know I'm just joking, Emily. I was just horrified about the robbery, and then when y'all decided to leave and be rice farmers I thought I might never see you again. But here you are and I'm so glad." Mercille doesn't usually gush, but her excitement at seeing her friend again is genuine.

The two women hug, and Mercille continues, "Come on in and find you a comfortable place to sit while I fix our coffee." Her house is very small and Emily can soon hear her bustling around in the tiny kitchen, pouring water in the coffee pot. Emily flops down into the big easy chair and does her best to follow Mercille's instructions to "make herself comfortable," wondering if that's really possible in her present expectant condition. In fact, it's hard for her to remember the last time she has been really comfortable; weeks, if not months ago, for sure.

She looks around the familiar room as she awaits the promised coffee, which is already beginning to send out a tantalizing aroma from the kitchen. Mercille's little house is always immaculate and the minute Emily settles in the big chair she recognizes the scent of fresh lemons that is so characteristic of this place. It's small, but pleasant and tasteful; typical of the times—not quite shabby, but certainly not dowdy. Nothing has changed; if she can be comfortable anywhere today, this is the place.

Mercille returns bearing the customary silver tray with the little rose-sprigged china coffee cups and demitasse spoons. There are even little linen napkins and cheese straws on the tray. "Well, now, when is this baby due, Emily? Late March? That's only a month from now. And what about Edith Joy? Where is she today?"

"E-Joy is with her Aunt Mamie this afternoon, Mercille. I don't know what I'd do without Mamie. She's going to look after Edith Joy while I'm in the hospital with the new baby. Mamie loves playing grandma. She's busy crocheting booties and sweaters now. She won't get much done on that project this afternoon, though. Edith Joy is getting to be quite a handful. Oh, let me tell you about her latest escapade! She tried to go for a visit to the neighbors' house all by herself. I took my eyes off her for a second and she was gone. You'd think I could keep up with a 17-month-old, but no, the minute I turned loose of her hand she started to run, with me right behind her."

"Oh, Emily, It's a wonder we're not looking at the new baby right now. How could you possibly run in your condition? Oh, how funny! I wish I had been there to see it. Well, no, if I'd been there I guess I'd surely have been chasing her instead of you, wouldn't I?"

"Yes, yes, and you'd probably have given her a good swat on the bottom, which is what I should have done, but I couldn't keep from laughing once I'd caught my breath, just thinking about what a spectacle we made. Poor baby. She got her punishment anyhow. Before I caught her, she ended up flat on her face, trying to crawl under Mrs. Dranguet's fence. She'd have made it, too, if her clothes hadn't gotten caught on the fence. It scares me to death now to think about having two little ones to look after, and that time will be here soon. The baby's due March 25 and Dr. Dickson told me at my last visit that everything seems to be right on schedule."

"Is Edith Joy excited yet about having a baby brother or sister?" Mercille continues, without waiting for Emily to answer, "You know, sometimes I feel kinda bad about Marcia being an only child, no one to play with, but to be perfectly honest I don't know if I could manage two little ones. Anyhow, that's not gonna happen, now, of course. And I'm not sure I'd even want another one with this awful depression going on. It costs enough to clothe and feed just one."

"Yes, well. You're right about that. Sometimes I do get a little scared thinking about all of it; chasing one toddler is almost too much to handle. To answer your question, though, E-Joy seems happy enough about the new baby—right now. We'll just have to wait and see how she feels when the new one actually shows up. She seems to like the idea but of course she's really too little to know what it's all about."

"Emily, I just hope you can work things out so that you can live here in this neighborhood. It's really not a bad place to live; it's quiet and peaceful and you already know the neighbors."

"Mercille, you know I'd love living near you and Georgia and I know Edith Joy would have nice playmates. I hope we can make it work out that way. Bob likes the idea, too. We'll just have to wait and see what happens. But yes, yes! I'm all for it."

Yes! Our little family did settle down in that little tiny neighborhood, in the little town of Coushatta, where we lived in a little house that I loved until our family outgrew it. And we struggled through the depression and war and we celebrated when good things happened.

We loved God and our neighbors and tried to do the best we knew how, at least *most* of the time. That is what this book is about.

Joy, Neenie, Marcia, and Alexa   Circa 1940

CHAPTER 2

The Neighborhood

2015 Looking Back – Inklings of the Greatest Generation?

As I look back at my past from the perspective of an old person already experiencing retirement, I realize that I have spent my life living in one small community, and my entire childhood living in the same small neighborhood, among family and friends, some of whom were almost like family. It's been a good life. We've never had much money, or many material things. After all, I was born on the dawn of the "Great Depression". But we've been blessed with a way of life that many sacrificed and even died to preserve and pass on to future generations. It's not all been good, of course; life never is, never has been. But it produced what some are now calling the "greatest generation." I believe there is much in that life worth preserving. That is why I write about it now for my family.

The Little House

1934 – Our Family in the Little House

The best thing about Twitchell Street is there's always somebody fun to play with. There's lotsa good things, but that's the best of all. At the "little house" where I live there's two of us children, and that's my baby sister and me. She doesn't like for me to call her Baby Sister, but sometimes I forget and do it anyway. So when I say "Baby Sister", I mean my little sister, Alexa, who is still almost a baby but not quite. We have a mother we call Momnee and then there's Daddy and an aunt whose name is Aunt Howard that lives with us, too.

The biggest house on our street belongs to the Scheen family, and it's right across the street from our house. They don't have a very big family, though; it's just Mr. and Mrs. Scheen and their only child, Fred Jr., who live there. I never call them Mr. and Mrs. Scheen, of course. You see, there's something different about our neighborhood. The children on Twitchell Street are allowed to call the parents on this street by their first names.

Not all the grown-ups, only the parents, because that makes it seem more friendlier, or at least that's the way Momnee explained it to me.

I forgot to say that we call the daddy in the family Big Fred. He is pretty big, but that's not why we call him that. It's because there's two Freds in that family so we call one of them Big Fred and the other one Fred Jr. so we won't get 'em mixed up. Fred Jr. is the only child in that family, which is why he's kinda spoiled. Well, I think he's real spoiled, cause he has way more toys than he needs, and he has a pony, and a sled, too, and it hardly ever snows here. I like Fred Jr., even if he is spoiled and a little bit bossy. He's a nice friend and he lets me and the rest of us swing in his back porch swing and his back yard swing, too.

Fred Jr.'s mother is named Georgia. She's a nice, tall lady, but sometimes she gets mad at us kids and bawls us out. She doesn't always see the bad things Fred Jr. does, or maybe she just forgets to fuss at him. Georgia has a colored lady named Beulah who comes and cleans up and cooks. I forgot to say that Big Fred goes to work at the "Big Store" every day. It's really Stephens' Store but

Scheen House

lots of people call it the "Big Store". They sell just about everything there at that store; shoes and clothes and chicken feed and Daddy said they even have caskets to put dead people in, but I've never seen them.

Sometimes we go to Fred Jr.'s house to play, especially when we play cowboys and Indians, cause it's the biggest yard and Fred has a wagon and some other good outdoor toys, but we can play at any of the yards in the neighborhood because our neighbors are all friendly. We can even play in our front yard at night sometimes, under the street light, and that's prob'ly the most fun of all in the summer and fall, when it's hot in the daytime. There's a ditch we can play in when it rains in the summer and it's almost like havin' our own swimmin' pool.

The Marston family live in the house next door to the Scheens and they're the littlest family of all because there's just Marcia (who's two years older than me) and her mother, Mercille. I don't know how old the grown people are; they never tell you that and Momnee says we shouldn't ask because that's not polite. Marcia has a daddy, too, but he doesn't live with them; he lives around the corner on Clark Street with his mother, Miss Emmy. I guess that's because she has a bigger house. Marcia's daddy's name is Henry Marston and he brings them things like vegetables out of his mother's garden and boiled peanuts and eggs and stuff like that and he smokes a long, curvy pipe but not in the house.

The Hand family moved to Twitchell Street right next door to us, but when they first moved there not long ago they didn't have a house to live in. It was okay though, because they came in a kind of covered wagon that had all their stuff in it. Baby Sister thought it was a Gypsy wagon but it's not. Their daddy, John D., got busy and built them a real house and it didn't even take him very long. He planted them a garden, too, like ours, only bigger. Their mother, Lessie, works at the Welfare Office like our mother does. The Hands have three boys and one of them is even older than Marcia and Fred Jr. His name is Jack and he's too old to play with the rest of us; he told us so. But the other two are the same ages as Baby Sister and me. Their names are Billy and Pewee and we like playing with them even though they're boys.

That's all the people who live on Twitchell Street, and I guess if there were any more children we prob'ly wouldn't have time to play with them all anyhow. I'm sure glad we have good playmates on our street.

Grandparents in the Neighborhood

You might think there's not that much for us to do on Twitchell Street because it's such a small street. It only has four houses but there's really lots for us kids to do because so many grandparents live in this neighborhood. If we ever get bored on our street, we can always go to one corner or the other and visit some of those grandparents. Marcia's grandmother, Miss Ella, has pretty, white hair and wears pretty dresses and she lives in a house on Ruby Street that my mother calls a Victorian cottage and I like to visit her. Everything in her house seems kind of little and old, but pretty, just like Miss Ella. I get to drink "coffee-milk" with the grown-ups when I go for a visit and we drink out of tiny little cups and stir with tiny spoons. Sometimes she even serves us tiny little cookies. Miss Ella's house is right across from our cow lot and there's a big chinaberry tree in the cow lot that we really like to play in, too. We play lots of pretend things up high in that chinaberry tree. Marcia has another grandmother in the neighborhood who lives on Clark Street, which is right behind our street. Her name is Miss Emmy Marston and she's real old. She had Marcia's birthday party at her house last year.

Marcia is my best friend besides Robbie Sue. She's two years older than me so I may not be her best friend, but we do play together a lot. We hafta be kinda careful when we play, though, because all of Marcia's clothes are so pretty and she's not s'posed to get dirty. Her dresses look like the party dresses in my paper doll books and she always has the fanciest costumes of anybody in the dance recitals, so most of the time we just play movie stars so Marcia won't get dirty. She can tap dance real good, too; I can dance pretty good but Baby Sister and I had to quit taking dance lessons because it was too expensive. Besides, Momnee wants us to start taking piano instead. Marcia will never stop taking dance lessons because her mother, Mercille, wants her to win lots of beauty contests and be a movie star like Shirley Temple. I bet she will, too; she always does everything her mother wants her to. When we play movie stars, Marcia always gets to be Ginger Rogers but I guess that's only fair 'cause she really is the best dancer and she has pretty long curls. I like to pretend I'm Sonja Henie because I'd like to be an ice skater when I get big. They have pretty costumes, too.

Robbie Sue is just the same age as me. Her grandparents live in our neighborhood at the other end of Ruby Street and their names are Mr. Frank and Mrs. Sally Adams. Miss Sally is the most grandmotherly kind of person that I know of. She wears grandmother shoes and she lives in a grandmotherly kind of house, too. She has a clock on her mantel that looks real old and it goes "bong, bong." She wears longish flowerdy dresses with aprons and has gray hair that she wears in a bun. She's real nice and she always gives us tea cakes when we go to see her and sometimes she lets us pick flowers out of her yard to take home with us.

Before Momnee started working at the welfare office, she would take me and Baby Sister to visit Miss Sally and then we'd walk around in her yard and she'd give Momnee little baby plants to take home and plant in our yard. She has all kinds of flowers in her yard like sweet peas an' larkspur an' petunias an' hollyhocks that are so tall they almost reach up to her roof. I didn't tell anybody this, but I used to pretend she was my grandmother, 'cause I never have had any grandparents of my own; that's the truth an' it's real sad. Then when Robbie Sue got to be my best friend, that's when I found out Mr. and Mrs. Adams were really *her* grandparents, so I had to quit pretending, but I still get to go and visit them.

Fred Jr.'s grandparents, Dr. Davis and Miss Ruth, live in our neighborhood, too, but just barely. They live on Carroll Street, right next to the telephone office and kind of behind Mr. and Mrs. Adams, and we don't see them very much, thank goodness. Usually, we just see Dr. Davis when we're sick. But we do get to hear Dr. Davis' fox hounds howling a lot at night. Sometimes they howl all night long and Daddy doesn't like that a bit. I'm sure they're very nice grandparents, but Dr. Davis is a big, big man and he has a big booming voice and gives us shots when we're sick.

I guess since Lexa and I don't have any grandparents of our own, it's kind of nice that we have so many grandparent neighbors. Maybe I can be a grandmother some day when I get really, really old. I hope so.

Illustration by Ellen Gaddis Howell

The Little House

I'm just sittin' here in my special place today; it's my secret special place in our yard and it's kind of a hole in the hedge where I go when I want to think about things. Right now I'm thinkin' about our house. Our family lives here in The Little House on Twitchell Street right across from the Scheen family. When we first moved here I was too little to remember, but I don't think we felt all that crowded with just Momnee, Daddy, and me. My baby sister, Alexa, got born about the same time we moved here but she was too tiny to make us any more crowded than we already were. We had plenty of rooms, but they were all pretty little except for a sleeping porch that went all the way across the back of the house.

Way back before I started school Momnee went to work at the Welfare Office and our Aunt Howard, Daddy's sister, came to live with us and look after "Baby Sister" and me. It was then that our family began to have "growing pains," as Momnee called it, so we built a big living room onto The Little House. But we just kept on calling it The Little House, 'cause it is. Now it's my favorite room because it has a hardwood floor that's slippery and slidey and a fireplace and French doors that open out to a screened porch and terrace. When Momnee waxes that pretty new floor, she gives me a raggedy old towel and lets me slide up and down on it and that makes it shine, shine, shine; then when we build a fire in the fireplace that floor really shines. Sometimes when it's real cold, we build a big fire in the fireplace and turn off the lights and tell stories and sing songs and listen to the fire crackle and pop in the fireplace. Yep, that's a lotta fun. Now Alexa and me have the old living room for our bedroom. Our house is a little bigger but it's still little enough to call it The Little House, and I like it that way.

Momnee doesn't have to work on Saturdays anymore and now she can do one of the things she likes to do the most of all and that is to plant flowers. It's hard work and sometimes she even lets me help, but mostly Nig helps her with the hard stuff like digging the big, big holes to plant trees and things like that. Nig is Crippled Sarah's husband. Sarah comes to our house and irons the clothes for us; she and Nig are just the nicest people and they have a daughter named Liza. Nig works in our garden, too, but on Saturdays he mostly helps Momnee with her flowers. Momnee tells me the names of all the flowers and then when I grow up, I'm gonna plant flowers and cultivate 'em like she does.

Joy, Alexa, and the Little House after it grew

Looking Back - After the War

When I was a child, I developed a strong attachment to The Little House. Not only did I love our house and yard; I loved the whole Twitchell Street Neighborhood as well. Momnee planted a dogwood tree out front, and crepe myrtles. We added a pecan tree, two peach trees, a pear tree, and a fig tree. Momnee also planted flowers of all kinds: roses, morning glories, sweet peas, Shasta daisies, chrysanthemums, and so many others. There was almost always something blooming. She taught me all their names, and I learned to love the flowers and the very thought of growing them myself someday.

I hoped I would have a green thumb like Momnee when I grew up. The things she grew always thrived. I'll never forget the horrible day we came home from church to find that our neighbor's cow had gotten out of the pen and eaten Momnee's little dogwood tree almost down to the ground. She cried, but she had the faith to leave it and it came back nice and bushy and bloomed better than ever the next year. That dogwood tree was living proof that Momnee had a green thumb, because it was planted right out in the blazing sun with no shade at all and in the springtime it was always one of the prettiest sights in the neighborhood. I really must give John D.'s cow her share of the credit too, because the pruning she gave it didn't hurt a bit.

I loved everything about the place where we lived, even the cow pen with its small shed at the back of our lot. We called it the barn, but it was too small to be a real barn; just a shed for the hay and a stool for Daddy to sit on when he milked the cow and a chicken yard nearby. We had a vegetable garden at one corner of the lot. Almost everybody in our little town had a cow and a garden; during the war we called our gardens "victory gardens," but I think they had more to do with keeping us from starving during the Depression years.

There was also a little car shed with tiny, pink Dorothy Perkins roses that crawled their way all over the top and sides, almost covering it completely on three sides. We later learned to call it a carport, but it was really just a shed; a beautiful pink shed during the blooming season. It was not attached to the house, but it did protect the car from the sun and rain.

I loved playing outdoors with the neighborhood kids in our yard and all over the neighborhood in summer, winter, fall, and spring. The most fun of all was playing outdoors on summer nights under the big street light between our house and the Hands. Baby Sister and I caught lightning bugs in jars by the thousands and put them on our bedside table for lanterns after we turned out the lights, but we set them free in the morning (if they were still alive). We even played out in the rain if there was no lightning, and when the ditches filled with rain water, it was almost like having our own swimming pool.

I loved the small open patch right across from Marcia and Mercille's house where the clover grew so thick that you could lie down on it like a bed and then sit up and make clover chains that would string all the way across the street. When we got tired of clover chains, we'd look for four leaf clovers until each of us had found at least one. We kids felt very lucky to live on Twitchell Street in a little house and a neighborhood like ours; at least, I know I did.

The Sleeping Porch

My favorite room in The Little House was not a regular room; it was the big back porch that stretched the entire width of the house and was screened on three sides. The original purpose was to provide a cool sleeping place for the hot summer months, but as our family expanded, we easily made the transition from sleeping porch to

Joy and Alexa in front of the sleeping porch

all-purpose, all-weather, all-season room. Heavy canvas curtains were rolled down to keep out the rain and the worst of the cold during the winter. Soon, Daddy put in a big, boxy, tin gas heater that kept the area reasonably warm, so our sleeping porch was used year-round, almost like today's family rooms, without the TV, of course. (There was not even a radio. It had its own special place in the living room.)

Two oscillating buzz fans, large shade trees, and southwesterly breezes kept the area as cool as could be expected during the long, hot Louisiana summers. It was a good spot to shell peas, churn, or do the ironing on scorching summer days. At night, the three beds made a much cooler place to sleep than the tiny, hot little bedrooms. Alexa and I could look out at the stars and count the lightning bugs that flashed their little lights at us as they flew by outside, close enough to touch. We could hear the cicadas and the tree frogs serenading us from the back yard.

This was the place where Momnee often read poems and sang songs to us, too, in the dark. One was called "Winken, Blinken, and Nod," and there was "Little Orphan Annie" and "The Raggedy Man." The one I liked best, though, was a popular song of the day that went like this:

> Red sails in the sunset, way out on the sea;
> Please carry my loved one home safely to me.

In winter, the snuggest, coziest place to be was in front of the big heater on the sleeping porch. When it

rained, we rolled down the canvas curtains and got on
the beds and pretended they were ships tossed about in
a rainy, stormy sea; sometimes our ships got wrecked.
We built wigwams by stretching quilts between chair
backs. With the rain drumming down on the tin roof
of the porch, we felt snug and safe and warm as could
be in our wigwam with our Indian babies in our arms.
We sang to them about the Indian maid called "Red
Wing". Sometimes at night Momnee rocked one of us
as she sang:

Oh, the moon shines tonight on pretty Red Wing;
The wind is sighing, the night bird crying...

One end of the sleeping porch became a playroom.
Our toys were stashed in a window seat near the door to
the kitchen. On cold winter days, this is where we often
played with our dolls, Emilie and Annette—two of the
famous Dionne quintuplets—and with our imaginary
playmates, Ruth and Louise. We had heard about the
Canadian quintuplets on the radio. Ruth and Louise were
almost as real to us, for a while, as our real neighborhood
playmates on Twitchell Street. Santa had brought us the
dolls, at our request, dressed in their furs and muffs for
the Canadian winter. Most of the time it was much too
warm for them to wear fur in Louisiana, but they got
used to it. I'm sure they did.

CHAPTER 3

Twitchell Street: A Place to Play, Grow, Celebrate

A Time to Play

"IT'S A BRAND spankin' new day." That's what Aunt Howard or any of the grown-ups would say, and Baby Sister and I are sittin' out here in the back yard playin' in the mud. I just like the way it feels when it squishes through my fingers, in little squiggles, all cool an' satiny like Momnee's nightgown; like butter feels 'cept you're not s'posed to play with butter, cause it's food. Food is expensive (that means it costs a lot of money), and lots of poor people don't even have enough to eat every day. So in the summertime we get to play in the mud.

Baby Sister has a worried look on her face. She doesn't talk very much cause she's a lot younger than me, but she thinks a lot and she worries a lot, too. If Daddy was here he'd prob'ly say to her, "What's goin' on underneath those golden curls, Alexa Earle? You worried about somethin'?" That's what he says when she gets scared. I bet she's scared

Aunt Howard's gonna be REAL MAD when she sees all this mud on our nice clean sunsuits she just put on us.

I don't worry about stuff like that. Aunt Howard takes care of us every day while Momnee goes to work at her office, and she fusses at us a lot more than Momnee; sometimes she kinda yells at us, but I don't care. I'd be sad if Momnee did that, but she never would. I like Aunt Howard okay, but I'm glad she's not our mother like Momnee is.

It's a good thing she came to live with us, though, so Momnee can go to work at her office every day, 'cause we need more money now that Daddy doesn't have his store anymore. One night some robbers came and took everything out of his store, so he doesn't have anything left to sell. Momnee says things like that happen when it's a depression. But we're not really poor. We have a cow and chickens and a garden, so you see, we always have something to eat. We have a pear tree, too, right here in the back yard with pears on it, but they aren't ripe yet. It's a tall tree an' we can climb in it, but I don't like to. I guess it's cause I'm kinda afraid. But Lexa loves to climb, an' she does it all the time; I wonder why she's not afraid to be up so high, but she's afraid of cows

Illustration by Ellen Gaddis Howell

and bridges. I guess there are different ways to be afraid, and different ways to be brave. People are all different in some ways, I guess.

Uncle Remus Is Alive On Twitchell Street, *1934*

Today I have mud in my eyes and it burns. I did have mud all over me but Aunt Howard won't let me come in the house like that. She made Fred Jr. squirt the hose on me until I'm almost clean. I'm glad it's a hot day. The water doesn't feel cold hardly at all; it just tickles. Aunt Howard is just shakin' her head and sayin' my sunsuit will never be the same again. Now I have to go indoors and take a bath; I hardly ever have to take a bath in the daytime but this time is different and Aunt Howard prob'ly already has the bath water on the stove gettin' hot. The worst part is now she's gonna scrub my ears and wash my hair, too. Soap will get in my eyes and that burns real bad. The reason for all this commotion so early this mornin' is all because of a story about "Brer Rabbit and a Tar Baby."

I don't know who read Marcia and Fred Jr. that story about Brer Rabbit and the tar baby but because of that ole story Aunt Howard is mad, MAD at me and she'll tell Momnee about what happened. The good part is that Momnee won't be as mad at me as Aunt Howard is. She'll prob'ly jus' sit me down and explain it to me and tell me not to ever do it again. She doesn't need to worry about that cause I like to play in the mud but I sure don't like havin' it all over me, and that's exackly what happened.

I didn't think a tar baby was a very good thing to be but I have to do whatever the bigger kids say, because—well, because they're bigger than me. It was kind of fun at first when they rubbed that cool, slippery mud all over my legs and arms and back but when they got to my face and hair it was kind of expiring.

When Fred Jr.'s mother, Miz Georgia Scheen came out the front door and saw me she just about fell out laughin.' She said all she could see of me was the whites of my eyes and then she sent Fred Jr. to get Aunt Howard and she even kinda laughed a little bit and she never laughs at the bad stuff we do. Most of the time Lexa and me don't mind doing what the older ones tell us. They think of some fun things to do; but sometimes their ideas are not so good for *us*.

Like another time when we were playin' at Fred Jr.'s house with his red wagon. (He has lots of good things to play with.) Fred Jr. and Marcia were playing cowboys, and the Indians were comin'. He said, "Look, they're fixin' to scalp y'all. Run quick and get in the wagon. I'll cover you up with this blanket so they can't find you and scalp you." A course we didn't really like having that hot blanket over us but we *had* to do it or else they wouldn't let us play. It got hotter and hotter under that blanket and sweat was runnin' into my eyes.

"Do you think maybe they forgot about us?" Lexa asked, after we'd been under that blanket a while. Her face was beginnin' to get red and a little bit sweaty.

"I don't think so, but it's dad-blamed hot under here; I'm gettin' outta here", I said. ("Dad-blamed" is one of Daddy's cuss words I like to use, but I can't do it when he's around.)

I was just fixin' to throw off the blanket, but Lexa said, "No, no, not yet! They'll make us quit playin' and go home." And I knew she was right.

Then we heard somethin' that made us forget all about that game and the wagon and all. We heard the sound of the ice man cloppin' down the street with his horse and wagon and then stoppin' right in front of our house like he always does. (We have an icebox in our kitchen to keep the milk cold.) Finally we just couldn't stand it anymore. We could hear him chippin' off the big block of shivery-cold ice to take into our kitchen. Well, that did it! We sure didn't want to miss out on those nice chunks of ice we knew he was gonna give us like he always does. We jumped out of that wagon faster'n a toad frog on a June bug, and ran to line up behind Fred Jr. and Marcia at the ice wagon. By that time we didn't even care if they got mad at us or not. The next thing that happened was real exciting for our whole neighborhood and kinda hard to explain, but I'll try. It went something like this:

Georgia had been watchin' out of her kitchen window that day when her only child Fred Jr. put us in that red wagon of his. She came stompin' out on her front porch and yelled real loud, "Fred Jr., you get that wagon out of the street. Those little girls could get run over!" Well, of course he just kept on playin' like he always does. The exciting thing was that a little later the laundry truck came around the corner and went "BAM, CRASH!" right over Fred Jr.'s wagon. The noise was so loud that Georgia came runnin' out on her porch again. When she saw that crumpled up wagon she just got hysterious and started screamin', "Oh, those children; those children!" so loud she couldn't even hear us tellin' her that we didn't get killed. She was watchin' when Fred Jr. put us *in* the wagon, but she didn't see the part where we got *out*. (She's kind of like that; sometimes she just doesn't even see the bad things he does).

Boy, that time she was *real* mad at him, though. I could tell because she was kind of shakin' all over and ringin' her hands. Lexa got a sad look on her face and said, "Poor Fred Jr.! His Mama is really mad at him this time." Lexa's so kind-hearted she was 'fraid he was gonna get punished real bad; but he *didn't*.

"Don't worry about him," I told her. "You know Georgia and Big Fred will just buy him another wagon." And that's exackly what they did. Big Fred brought him one home from L.P. Stephens & Co. the very next day.

Maybe one of these days we'll get big enough to not have to do everything the big kids tell us to. But now, today I'm gonna hafta take a bath in hot, hot water and let Aunt Howard scrub my ears hard and wash my hair and get soap in my eyes. She'll even have to brush my hair and get the tangles out, and that *hurts*! But I'm just glad we didn't get killed by that ole laundry truck the other day, and if Momnee ever asks us if we'd like to hear a book written by somebody named Uncle Remus, I think I'll say, "No, thank you!"

Two Little Sisters

I like to talk to my baby sister, Alexa, about things I think about, while we're cuttin' paper dolls out of the new paper doll books Momnee brings us from Shre'port. Well, ackshully I'm doing most of the cutting because Lexa is still pretty little; she's just 4 years old and I'm almost six. But she's real smart for somebody that little and she likes to play paper dolls even if she can't cut 'em out too good. Sometimes she accidentlly cuts their heads off and that makes her cry.

She cries about a lot of stuff but I guess that's just because she's so little. I sure hope that's it because it bothers me when she cries and I wish she'd just get over that.

Joy and Alexa

Lexa never complains about the food we have to eat. If Aunt Howard puts somethin' on her plate she doesn't like, she just does something sensible. Like puttin' her liver in the sugar bowl when nobody's looking. I wish I could think of things like that. She hardly ever gets in trouble.

She's still a baby in some ways even if she doesn't want to be called "Baby Sister." For one thing she's such a scaredy-cat. She's scared to death of animals! Mostly she's scared of the big ones like cows and horses and tigers. I think it would be cruel to take a child like her to the circus.

As big as I am, I still get kinda scared when Aunt Howard threatens to call the sheriff. Yep, she says, "Oh, Lordy mercy. If y'all don't quit that squabblin' I'm gonna call the sheriff to y'all." But of course she never does it. (I don't think they put children in jail. I sure hope not.)

Lexa's 'fraid of bridges, too. Sometimes when we're

ridin' in the car and we come to rickety ole wooden bridges Daddy has to stop and let her walk across and I have to get out and hold her hand and walk with her so she won't cry.

Lexa has to tag along with me just about everywhere I go now. I try to take good care of her so she won't get scared when we go to new places like birthday parties. Of course she won't have to go to school with me but just about everywhere else she does.

One day not long ago Momnee got Daddy to drive us to Sunday School at the Methodist Church, which is right across from my real school. Well, here we go with her taggin' along holding onto me just like I'm her mama. We get to the big tall steps going up to the main front door of the church, but when we pull on the door handle that big ole door won't open and then we don't know what to do.

"I see another door over here," I whisper to Lexa. She doesn't say a single word. Her eyes just look bigger than ever an' real scared. I'm just hoping she won't start crying and embarrass me to death. Then the next thing I know she starts pulling on my sleeve real hard.

"What is it?" I ask her.

"I don't see anybody," she whispers.

Right then a kind of a revolution from God comes to me. "Oh, no!" I'm thinking. If there's nobody here that means they're not having church. I know

First Methodist Church Coushatta

it's Sunday because the big Sunday funny papers already came. And besides, Daddy wouldn't let us out of the car if it wasn't Sunday. So if it's Sunday and they're not having church that means they've prob'ly already had church before we got here. We're too late. (We're always being late to places because we have a new baby at home.)

"I think now we'll walk home," Lexa says and she turns around and starts walking before I can even say, "Okay," or "shut up," or anything. (Of course I don't say "shut up" to her, because Momnee doesn't allow us to say ugly words like that.)

When we get home nobody's even mad at us. They just kinda laugh and explain that we're mistakened about church. It's not over after all. We were just a little bit early. (I don't know how that could happen to us.) Lexa tells me now that she knew all the time that we were early but she didn't say anything because she was ready to go home. Can you believe that?

I really love my little sister but sometimes I have a hard time liking her all that much. She just gets by with so much stuff and still people keep on thinking she's so cute, so darling, and so beautiful with her big brown eyes and golden curls and all that. She stays quiet most of the time because she knows how grown-ups like for children to act. Going by what I already know about Lexa I think when she starts to school she's gonna do just fine if she doesn't have too many things to be scared of at school and if she doesn't get a mean teacher. I think having a mean teacher would just about kill her.

Well, most teachers are not really mean and even a mean teacher prob'ly wouldn't be mean to Lexa. But if the teacher was mean to other kids—'specially poor ones or sick or crippled ones like Tiny Tim in that Christmas story it would just about break her heart.

I'm glad I have a little sister and I love her and I even like her most of the time.

My Favorite Place

I'm seven years old now; I might as well say that right away and get it over with 'cause that's what everybody always wants to know about. I'm prob'ly too old to be out here playin' in the mud, but it's hot this mornin' and I'm sittin' on the cool, bare ground between our house and the hedge. I have on my yellow playsuit and I can feel the damp ground soak through my clothes and it feels good. The leaves in the silver maple tree get all glittery every time the wind shakes 'em, and when I look up high over my head the sky is bright blue without even one little cloud.

This is my favorite place. This tree is right next to the hedge and there's a hole just the right size for me. When I was real little I used to think this was where God lived because if I sat here for a while I thought I could hear him whispering to me and telling me he loved me but it was prob'ly just the wind in the maple tree over my head. I could crawl through this hole right now into the Hands' backyard. I could yell kind of loud and Billy and Pewee Hand would come out to play but I want to wait a while. Sometimes it's more fun just to do things by myself, like makin' this toad frog house. I'm diggin' it with a big kitchen spoon and Aunt Howard will prob'ly be mad about that, but it sure does dig good. This house has lotsa rooms and it's gonna be real big by the time I get finished with it.

I might even dig a swimmin' pool for the frogs. Sometimes Momnee takes us to Natchitoches to the pool there, but not very often. It's a long ways from Coushatta. I bet the frogs will like havin' a place to swim. I sure wish we had a swimmin' pool in our yard. Sometimes we talk about diggin' one but I don't think we could really do it.

It's fun diggin' frog houses. They don't have to have hardly any furniture. Just some sticks for benches 'cause the frogs don't ever sit on 'em anyway. About all they do is hop up and down and try to get out. We have to put sticks across the top for a roof so they can't get out. Lexa thinks that's real sad. She says the houses are more like jails than houses. Oh, well, we don't keep our toad frogs very long because there's lots of 'em and they're fun to catch so we just get us some new ones every time and let the old ones go.

"You didn't wait for me!" Lexa's voice scares me because most of the time she's real quiet but this time I don't even see her 'til she touches my arm. She's a quiet kind of person.

"Hey, that's a nice frog house you made. It has lotsa rooms. It must be for a family, but it still looks kinda like a jail," she says. She just can't seem to get over that.

"Yeah, but I might dig 'em a swimmin' pool, though," I tell her. "And I betcha jails don't have swimmin' pools.

I betcha they'd like these houses we make for 'em if they had swimmin' pools."

"Oh, that's a good idea," she says, and then she sees the big kitchen spoon I'm usin.' "Ooh, ooh, you're gonna be in *big trouble*! That's one of the good cookin' spoons." Her eyes get huge when she says that. She may be little, but she knows how Aunt Howard is about stuff like that.

"I'm almost through with it," I tell her. "I just thought of another good idea. I'll let you dig the swimmin' pool if you want to. While you're diggin' I'll go in and get a little pan of water to wash the spoon with and we can pour the rest of the water in the pool. Then we can catch our toad frogs and let them swim in the pool." (I think this is one of my best ideas I've ever had.) Lexa starts diggin' while I go inside to get the water.

Soon as I open the screen door I can smell dinner cookin' and it smells good. There's pork chops sizzlin' in the skillet, so I know we'll have rice and gravy, too. We eat rice a lot 'cause Momnee grew up on a rice farm and she really loves it. Mary hasn't started makin' the pies yet, but pretty soon our kitchen will be prob'ly the busiest place in town. Every day but Sunday, our cook, Mary, makes the food for the plate lunches that Daddy serves at his Loreco Café. Lucky for me everybody is pretty busy so they won't pay much attention to me.

"Is it okay if I get a pan of water to take outside, and a big spoon?" I say to nobody in particular and then Mary just says, "Okay, baby. Now get out of this kitchen; we've got lots of cookin' to do."

When I get back outside with the pan of water, Lexa's almost through with the swimmin' pool. I finish it real quick and wash the big spoon. I dry it on the top part of my sunsuit 'cause the bottom part's a little dirty. I pour the water into the pool and then I back up a little bit so I can see the outcome. It looks pretty good. Then I send Lexa back to the kitchen with the pan and spoon and nobody is the wisest. But when she gets back outside all the water has just soaked right into the ground. No swimmin' pool!

Oh, well, we're tired of makin' toad frog houses anyway so everything's workin' out pretty good and we're not even in trouble this time. Now we can call Billy and Pewee to come over and play in the big chinaberry tree. Everybody in the neighborhood likes to play in that tree. At least, all of us kids do. It's my very favoritest place to play.

Pal and Ginger – Can Bird Dogs Be Pets?

Daddy has always had bird dogs as far back as I can remember but Pal and Ginger are the only ones I ever got to know personally. You can tell Daddy doesn't like them all that much because of the way he talks about them when he comes home from hunting. One day I heard him say, "If I ever buy another damned Irish Setter, I hope somebody will kick my behind".

(I'm not allowed to talk like that, but anyway that's how I found out they're Irish Setters.) Daddy is never mean to his dogs but you can just tell he doesn't have much respect for them. Maybe that's because they're Irish, but that doesn't seem right; after all, our family has Irish blood, too.

Momnee says it's not right to treat people bad just because of their color or nationality or the church they go to. That's called "prejudice" and I think it might be a sin. Daddy seems to be prejudiced about those dogs, and sometimes about people too. But Momnee *never* is.

I love those dogs. They're so pretty. They have long, silky hair.

My dog is named Pal and he's prettier than Lexa's dog. We have arguments about whose dog is the best, but it doesn't matter because I know mine is. Pal has a white background with black spots on him about the color of Momnee's hair. He's a happy kind of dog. He's always running and jumping and almost knocks me down sometimes, but he's lots of fun to play with.

Lexa's dog, Ginger, has hair about the color of mine and she's sort of quiet and calm and nice like Alexa. I think maybe Ginger has a lot on her mind; maybe she worries about things. I'm glad our dogs don't bark all the time like some dogs do. Dr. Davis's fox hounds bark all night long and wake people up and Daddy gets mad.

Pal and Ginger must be married to each other because guess what! Ginger gave us the best surprise on Mothers' Day. She had thirteen puppies! Daddy didn't seem very surprised, and he said we would need to find good homes for them. I was hoping he would let us keep the whole litter and I told him I'd help with them, but Daddy said, "No," and he doesn't usually change his mind.

Those puppies are so cute and wiggly and their eyes are just beginning to open up. You should see when Ginger feeds them, all at the same time. They squirm around and completely cover her up.

One day Daddy brought his friend, Mr. Bunk Andrews, who is the Counting Agent, over to look at them. I guess because there were so many. He had his little girl, Annette, with him so she could pick out a puppy to keep. She is even littler than me and I'm sure she's not old enough for a puppy. It's a big responsibility.

Annette, was looking them over, and petting them. And I just held my breath and prayed that she wouldn't pick the one I named Heidi.

She just kept looking and looking and then, finally – thank goodness, she picked one I hadn't even named yet! I wish we could keep just one or two puppies, but Daddy said, "No," and he really doesn't change his mind. I sure am gonna miss those puppies.

The Dungeon

Janie Carol Barrett lives not far from us but she hardly ever comes to our neighborhood to play. She's not as old as me; she's about the same age as Lexa. Maybe the reason she doesn't play with us much is because her mother thinks we're bad. That's prob'ly it. One day she called Momnee on the phone and said, "Your kid stole my kid's lunch kit." Well, Momnee knew that wasn't true, because we don't steal things and we don't even eat lunch at school, but everybody got over all that and Janie Carol is here today and we're playin' with her, but we're not havin' much fun. She's not havin' much fun either. I think it's prob'ly because she likes to play more with toys and we mostly like to make up our own games. Here she comes now.

"It's hot out here. Don't y'all ever play in the house?" she asks.

"Not much," I tell her. "There's not all that much to do in the house but play paper dolls," I explain. "We could play paper dolls if you want to," I tell her.

"Paper dolls!" Then she makes a pouty face and says, "I don't like to play paper dolls at all. That's no fun anyhow."

Well, that just about takes the cake. All my friends like to play paper dolls. I'm beginning to think Janie Carol is just not a very enjoyable person. "Well, what would you like to play?" I ask her.

"I wanta play with your toys," she says, (like paper dolls aren't toys!) "I wanta go in the house 'cause it's too hot out here. I'd rather play in the house." Well, I can tell right away that this isn't gonna be a real good day.

"Janie Carol, if we go in the house now, some of the grownups will prob'ly say, 'if you kids can't find anything to do outdoors, then you can help shell peas,' or somethin' like that." Well, she makes a worse pouty face than ever and puts her hands on her hips. And then I remember that she's an only child like Fred Jr. only poutier, so I'll just hafta look over it and be nice to her because she's company. I guess she's just bored.

Just then who should come runnin' across the street but Fred Jr., himself. "Hey, Janie Carol," he says, "what are you doin' over here on our street?"

She looks at him like you would look at an ole bug. "Well, it's a free country, ain't it? I came over here to play, but there's nothin' to do, and it's too hot to stay out doors," she says in a whiney voice.

I know you're s'posed to be nice to people when they're company, but I get tired of tryin' to be nice to Janie Carol, she's so much trouble. I guess I'm just not used to her.

Well, about that time Billy and Pewee come out their front door and Fred Jr. says, "Hey, I just thought of a good thing we can play. We can play King Arthur and his Knights of the Round Table."

That sounds like a good idea to me, but Janie Carol is still kinda pouting. "What in the world is that?" she asks. "I don't think I ever heard of it, and I sure don't know how to play it."

"Oh, it's easy," Fred Jr. starts to explain, but Billy Hand has just stepped off his front porch and yells out, "I know, I know! The boys get to be King Arthur and the knights; the girls get to be the princesses and get rescued from the cruel dragon."

"Yep, that's it," says Fred Jr. as he nods his head, but then he gets a thoughtful look on his face. "No, I'm not sure we can play this game," and this time he shakes his head from side to side. "Nope, if we play this we'll have to let Janie Carol see our 'Secret Dungeon' and then it won't be a secret anymore."

"Well, that ain't exackly fair," Janie Carol says and you can see she's mad this time for sure. "If all of y'all know about it, then it's not that much of a secret so why can't I, if I promise not to tell?"

"Oh, I don't think so," Fred Jr. shakes his head again. "You might forget and tell your mama or somebody."

"I promise and cross my heart and hope to die, I ain't gonna tell nobody if you'll let me see it." (I think that's when Janie Carol quit bein' bored.)

Next thing that happens, Marcia comes over and there are too many princesses so I get to be the dragon. Fred Jr. is King Arthur, of course, and the others are knights or princesses. Then I count to ten while everybody hides just like in reg'lar old "hide 'n' seek." I try to find a princess to haul off to the dungeon, which is really the Hands' storm cellar. Then the other princesses find a knight and tell him to go rescue her.

The dragon, who is me, stands guard by the door to the dungeon. When the knight comes we'll have a sword fight and try to slew each other. That's the best part. I've seen lots of Errol Flynn movies so I'm a pretty good sword fighter; course it's just pretend.

There aren't any real rules to this game; we mostly just do everything as much like in the picture shows as we possibly can. I catch Marcia first. Of course King Arthur himself comes to rescue her. She's the most beautiful princess of all. As soon as our sword fight is over I revive and go to find Janie Carol. (We all know not to find Lexa. She'll get too scared and worried about spiders and snakes in the dungeon, so we just skip over her for this part.)

When I finally find Janie Carol she says, "I've changed my mind. I don't care about seeing any old storm cellar dungeon."

"Are you sure?" Fred Jr. asks her. "It's nice and cool in there, and this may be your only chance to see it."

"Scaredy-cat, scaredy-cat! You're just a titty baby." (I don't know who said that, but it surely wasn't me. We're not allowed to say things like that in our family.) Poor Janie Carol. I 'm startin' to feel a little bit sorry for her now.

"I ain't no scaredy-cat!" she yells back. "You're a liar, liar, pants on fire, Fred Jr. Scheen!"

Why do I even feel sorry for Janie Carol? It just doesn't pay to feel sorry for some people. Anyway, I'm beginning to think she can take care of herself pretty well.

"Well, prove it, then! Prove you're not scared." Fred Jr. is the oldest and biggest and kind of the boss, except when Marcia persuades him to be nice.

Marcia has already gone home though, a few minutes ago, because it was time for her to go to her dance lesson. So I guess Fred Jr. decides this is a good time to not be nice.

"Come on, prove it," he taunts. "All you have to do is go down those stairs to the storm cellar one time and we'll know you're not scared."

Everything gets quiet. Fred Jr. is waiting. Janie Carol still doesn't say anything. Finally, Fred Jr. can't stand it any longer. (The rest of us are all getting kind of tired of this game.)

"Okay," he says, "now we know you're a 'scaredy cat' cause even Pewee's not scared to go down there when he gets caught, and he's littler'n you are."

Well, o' course Peewee isn't scared. It's his own house and his own storm cellar, and his own jars of canned peaches in there, but I guess maybe Janie Carol hasn't thought about that. Poor girl! Now I really feel sorry for her, and I'd of been even more sorry if I hadda known what was goin' to happen next.

It's a big surprise to all of us. Even Fred Jr. is surprised. Janie Carol just marches down those steps like she's been doin' it all of her lifetime, and when she gets to the bottom, Fred Jr. slams the door shut. He really doesn't know it will lock; he just wants to scare her a little, not lock her up. None of us know, not even Billy and Pewee. And none of us know how to unlock it.

Janie Carol lets out a blood-curdlin' yell. "Help! No fair! Get me out of here! It's all dark in here." And then she starts beatin' on the door and screamin'. At that very minute we all realize we're in trouble.

"Y'all, what're we gonna do?" asks Fred Jr. "It's not gonna be just Janie Carol's mother that's mad this time. All our mothers are gonna be furious at us."

I'm scared. Not as scared as Janie Carol, prob'ly, but maybe even scareder than Lexa, for once.

Fred Jr.'s standin' real close to the door now and talkin' to Janie Carol. "Just hush up screamin' for a minute and we'll find somebody that can get you out. Honest, we didn't know the door would lock."

"Well, well, well, what have we here?" A voice from behind us makes us all nearly jump out of our skins. It's John D. Hand, Billy and Peewee's daddy, lookin' down the cellar stairs at us with a big frown on his face. "Y'all think bad weather's on the way, huh? Needed to get in the storm cellar, huh?"

By now we're all lookin' down at our feet, not knowin' what in the world to say, and then Fred Jr. gets this look on his face like a light just came on and he says, "Yes, sir, there was this bad cloud just a few minutes ago, and . . ."

"Well, son, I just happen to have the key, and I'll be glad to let you in. How long you think you'll need to stay? Would any of the rest of you like to go in and stay in the storm cellar?"

"Oh, uh . . . No, sir, well actually, what happened was,

you see, sir, . . . well, we slammed the door by accident, and somebody got locked in there, and . . . uh, well we need to get her outta there, and then, . . . well, we uh . . . we need to go home, Mr. Hand."

"Oh, yes, I think I do see. Well, now, what can we do about this situation? If any of you'd like to stay awhile, just in case there's a storm brewin' out here . . . "

"NO, SIR. We've gotta go!" It's a chorus this time. Unanimous; no undecideds.

Janie Carol didn't venture back over to Twitchell Street again anytime soon. And none of us ever mentioned our adventure to anyone. It was over for good. Nobody's mother even phoned anybody. We were really tired of that game.

Playhouse in the Sky (1980's Looking Back)

It's summertime sometime in the 1980's, I'm an old lady now, and I have grandchildren visiting. They are curious about what my life was like when I was a little girl. "Mama Joy, did you ever have a real playhouse? I mean the kind you could really go inside and play in?" one of them asks. Suddenly, it's story time, again!

"Well, yes and no. In a way it was a real playhouse because it was built of wood, but in a way it was not as real as my imaginary playhouse because it didn't feel as much like a real house."

Now their curiosity is aroused. They want to know what I mean by that strange answer. So I tell them the following true story:

"Almost as far back as I can remember, the Twitch-ell Street bunch always had playhouses but you have to remember that all this happened way back during the "Depression days" of the 1930's when almost nobody had any money; so we had to be creative. We made playhouses outdoors out of anything we could get our hands on. Sometimes we raked up leaves in the back yard and made leaf boundaries for walls. Then we would find old boxes and wash tubs and buckets and use them for furniture. We would sneak tin pie pans and spoons out of the kitchen when Aunt Howard was not looking and use them for dishes. The good thing about leaf houses was that when you got tired of playing house you could always run and jump and roll in the leaves.

"When we played indoors, Alexa and I could make beautiful dollhouses in the front bedroom. This game was inspired by two miniature china figurines about 5 inches tall that Momnee brought us from one of her trips to Shreveport—from Woolworth's, probably. They were beautiful ladies, mine dressed in a green evening gown and Alexa's in blue. We tried to give them just the right elegant surroundings because they were so elegant themselves.

"I always built mine a grand 3-story house out of a 3-tiered table. A square marble ashtray turned upside down and set on three spools of thread made a lovely dining table. Big books were about the right size for beds, but we never used the Bible because we figured it would be a sin to use the Bible for something like that. We used fancy handkerchiefs and lace doilies for bedspreads and tablecloths. Two match boxes made a perfectly good chair when covered with velvet cloth from Momnee's scrap bag.

"Our doll houses were so beautiful it was sad not to be able to show them to anyone but we had to do all this in secret, and very quietly while Aunt Howard was napping or out back doing the wash. She would never have put up with such nonsense if she had known about it and when and if we did get caught we had to clean up all the mess, which took quite a while.

"One summer when Daddy was not as busy as usual with his regular job he decided to build us a real playhouse in the back yard. He said it could always be used as a washhouse when we were older. A friend helped him and when they got it finished it looked like a real house, with windows and a front porch with little benches on each end. It was so cute we couldn't believe our good fortune. We didn't have any furniture to go in it and somehow it looked too nice to put washtubs and cardboard boxes in it for furniture, so until we had some proper furniture we just kept playing in the house in our chinaberry tree in the cow lot.

"A few months went by and one day a big delivery truck pulled up in the yard. Two men got out and unloaded a washing machine with a wringer and two big tubs on a stand. Next thing we knew they were taking them up the steps to our playhouse. From that minute our playhouse took on a new life as a washhouse. At first we were fascinated watching the clothes swish around in the machine, then go through the wringer with its rubber rollers which could pull your fingers into it if they got too close; then into the rinse water and the bluing and back through the wringer again. We even asked to help with the laundry and enjoyed it for a while but our enthusiasm soon wore off and we found ways to avoid this chore. But that's another story.

"We never tired of playing in our chinaberry tree house. It was the best playhouse anyone could ever want. It was located across the road from the house where Marcia's grandmother, Miss Ella lived. It belonged to all the neighborhood kids and anyone else who happened to be visiting at the time. It was not a real house at all, not even a real tree house. There was not a single board to be found anywhere in it and the only furniture existed in our imaginations. But each of us had our own limb, which sometimes served as a room, and sometimes served as a whole house. Sometimes it was a fort where we threw chinaberries at each other. It could even be an office like the one where Momnee and Mrs. Hand worked.

"Our favorite pastime of all was when our chinaberry tree playhouse became a radio station, and we conducted radio broadcasts from that cool, lofty spot on warm, sunny days. Marcia liked to be the announcer and we all sang and did ads for products you've never heard of, like Palmolive Soap and Pond's Cold Cream and Tangee Lipstick. Marcia could make her voice sound soft and romantic when she talked about Evening in Paris Perfume.

"We spent many happy summer mornings and fall afternoons high in the chinaberry-tree house. When neighbors passed by we hid so they couldn't see us in our secret place. Sometimes they waved anyway. We felt safe and secure in the branches of that old tree, cut off from the rest of the world." I paused for a moment; this seemed like a good ending for my tale.

"And then what happened? What else did you do? Please tell us the rest. Please, please!"

"Well, one day when we were singing a rousing chorus of 'ninety-nine bottles of beer on the wall' from our perches there was a loud cracking sound and a rustling of leaves and branches. Alexa's limb had broken and came crashing down as she tumbled head-over-heels onto the back of our unsuspecting milk cow, Daisy, who up to that unfortunate moment had been grazing peacefully under our tree—enjoying the music I suppose. Daisy was not amused by this rude interruption and let it be known by giving a small leap, an indignant toss of her head and trotting unceremoniously toward her shed, head in the air, eyes bulging, and bawling at the top of her lungs. This was her cow pen and we were trespassing. Alexa, on the other hand, lay face down in the weeds, too terrified to move or make a sound.

"Fred Jr. was the first to recover from the shock. 'What're we gonna do, y'all?' Marcia had a worried look on her face, 'I hate to say this but I think she might be dead.' We began screaming all at the same time. I was crying too because I loved my little sister a lot even though she did make me mad sometimes.

"At about this time we saw Aunt Howard come running out the back door, hands in the air, shouting, 'Good Lord a'mighty! What have y'all done now? Well, this just takes the cake. Y'all know you're not s'posed to play in the cow pen. Now we won't get any milk a'tall. I oughta call the sheriff to y'all; c'mon inside and I'll give you somethin' to do. Y'all can shell peas for me. That'll keep you out of trouble for a while.' Then she spotted Alexa

Illustration by Ellen Gaddis Howell

lying face down in the tall grass. She began wringing her hands. 'Oh, lordy mercy, I'd better get Dr. Davis over here quick as I can. This child may be dyin' and I'm 'bout to have a heart attack, myself.'

"As it turned out, Alexa was all right; just shaken up a bit.

She was brave when it came to climbing trees but confronting animals, especially cows and horses, was a different matter. I think it was hearing Dr. Davis' name mentioned that brought her back to reality. We were all scared of him. We admired Alexa a lot after that because she awoke from the dead just in time to spare us from his big, booming voice and intimidating presence. The End."

"I liked that story, Mama Joy. 'Specially the part about Aunt Alexa and the cow. I'm glad it had a happy ending. Did you ever wish you had played in your other playhouse? Your real one? Did you feel sad about it?"

"Never did," I replied.

"Why not?" they persisted.

"I think it was because we never got tired of our china-berry house. I still think it was the best playhouse in the world; sort of a playhouse in the sky. It was just right for us, because when we used our imaginations that tree could be anything we wanted it to be, and we loved imagining things. If it had been happening today I suspect that the chinaberry tree would have been our Space Ship."

I think, in some strange way, our chinaberry tree house was the most real to us, and much more fun than any play-house we have ever had. After all, we built it ourselves, in our imaginations, and it could be anything to us, anytime. Maybe even a house on the planet Mars, who knows?

CHAPTER 4

Coushatta Grade School Days

1936 – Momnee, Please Don't Leave Me!

"I'M NOT SCARED, am I Momnee? I've been here before, haven't I?" It was my first day of school and I was scared.

"Of course you've been here," my mother replied. "I'm glad you remembered. It was when you took dancing lessons but that was more than a year ago. You're smart to remember that. I'll bet you remembered those big white columns on the front of the school, didn't you?"

"Yep, I did. I remember how loud the taps on my shoes sounded on that big concrete front porch. 'Specially when I went 'tap, shuffle, tap, tap' doin' The Darktown Strutters' Ball all by myself. An' I had on that black shiny costume with the short pants an' the funny-lookin' tails on the back an' the tall hat."

"You do remember a lot about dancing lessons. Dancing out on that big front entrance portico with all the other children. You had so much fun dancing, and I know you're going to like school. You'll make new friends and you'll learn a lot of new things; how to read books and write. You'll get to color with the new crayons we bought you."

"But you'll still read to me when I come home, won't you, Momnee? I like it when you read to me 'cause you put s'pression in it, and remember? I can already write my name.

Remember? Daddy taught me that. I wrote E-JOY 'cause that's what he calls me. And you said I did it real good; remember?"

"I do remember, and it *was* good but . . . " Momnee was trying to make me feel better about going to school here in this big building, but I'm still feeling scared all the way down to my tummy.

"Excuse me, Miss Emily, would you like me to take your daughter to her classroom for you? I'll bet you need to get to work, don't you?" Some kind of a teacher was holding out a hand to me and smiling at Momnee.

"Well, I . . . " Momnee began. The helpful lady looked at me. "Here, just hold onto my hand and I'll take you to meet your teacher. She's a very nice lady; her name is Miss Huggins."

I was just thinkin' what a nice name "Miss Huggins" is for a teacher, when the nice lady looked at me again and asked . . . "and what is *your* name?"

"My name is Edith Joy, but that's too long for most people to remember, so people usually just call me Joy, and this is my new school dress that Momnee made me and my new school shoes we just bought."

The nice lady kept holding onto my hand and she said, "Well, what lovely new school shoes, and you look so pretty in that new dress your mommy made you, Edith Joy."

This was a real nice lady; I could tell by the way she smelled all powdery and nice—like Momnee and my Sunday School teacher, Miss Beth Ogilvie. I thought this lady must be a teacher, too. She was smiling and she had a nice soft voice, but why was she whispering to Momnee now? Why did Momnee let go of my hand and walk toward the door?

I tried to grab Momnee's hand. "Momnee, please don't leave me," I begged. She knelt beside me and whispered, "Calm down; it won't be for very long. I have to go to work now, but I'll be back to get you soon." She kissed me and then she turned and walked out the door.

"NO! NO!" I screamed as I ran after her and pushed on the heavy front door of that school building. "No, Momnee, please don't leave me!"

It was too late I knew but still I had to try. The big front door slammed shut. I pushed with all my strength, ran out onto the porch with the great big columns, down the steps and into the schoolyard but it was no use. I don't even know who it was that caught me and brought me back in. I was barely aware of the stares of the other children and the way they laughed. I didn't care. I just knew that I had a panicky feeling in my stomach; I knew that I wanted my mother.

Momnee was right, of course. I did learn to like school; I loved the teachers, the new friends, coloring pictures and reading books all by myself. And she did still read to me lots of the long books that I couldn't read for myself; the books that I loved like *Heidi* and *The Little Lame Prince*, and *Anderson's Fairy Tales*. She came to school sometimes to bring cookies for parties and to see plays and other school programs that I was in. She joined the PTA and was president one year.

Looking Back

My first grade year got me off to an excellent start in school. My teacher, Miss Huggins (which was her real name) proved to be a first-rate teacher of young children. I cannot think of a single unpleasant thing that happened to me in her classroom and I probably remember more about that year than any other except my senior year in high school. I was totally excited about learning, and was happy being my teacher's unofficial helper that year;

Coushatta Grade School

reading just came natural to me, probably because I had been read to so much by my mother in the years before school. Miss Huggins let me help teach new words to the children who were not having such an easy start, and I enjoyed it. I also enjoyed being able to read real books all by myself. I also loved the coloring sheets, especially those with holiday themes. I don't know how many boxes of crayons I used up that year.

I only remember one slightly unpleasant thing that happened that year, and it did not happen in the classroom. It was customary in our school when we needed to use the toilet, to raise our hand and say, "I need to be excused to go to the basement." We were then allowed to leave the classroom and go alone outside the main building to one or the other of two small wooden structures located on the ground level directly behind the main building, one labeled BOYS and the other GIRLS. This procedure was a little daunting to me at first, because I knew what a basement was; at the church I attended on Sundays my Sunday School Class was located in the basement of the church and it was not a toilet. Once I adjusted my thinking to understand and accept this little discrepancy in word meanings I was able to go through that simple process of leaving to go to the restroom without the accompanying panic.

One day, after I had been properly excused from the classroom, I was making my way cautiously through the big hall, past the stairs and into the passageway to the side door on my way to the 'basement' when I heard the unmistakable slap of tennis shoe soles on the floor right behind me. When I turned to see who was there I was dismayed to recognize the big grin on the face of one of my first grade classmates, Wilber Gene Daily. Wilber Gene was not quite a bully, but was well on his way to becoming one, and would probably fit that description by third grade at the rate he was going. Continuing to grin, he calmly exposed the more private parts of his anatomy and laughed out loud while I decided not to scream and instead made the ugliest monster face at him I could and ran out the side door, around the corner of the building and into the girl's "basement." That was the first and last time that ever happened to me.

My school days were happy days and I had many happy times with Momnee helping me do all kinds of things. She helped me with homework sometimes and encouraged me (well, nagged is a better way to say it) to learn to play the piano. The best thing was I always knew I could count on her to be there when I needed her. That never changed.

Looking Back Again Much Later

Later, many years later, Momnee was ninety-one years old and in the hospital for the last time with congestive heart failure. I walked into her room and was struck by how small and frail she looked, and how our roles had reversed. It was like I was the mother and she the child. I walked over to the bed. She was sleeping soundly; should I wake her? She was sleeping so peacefully, but I knew she would want to see me; she always did.

A panicky feeling came over me and I was a five-year-old

again remembering that day so long ago and before I realized it I was whispering, begging, "Momnee, please don't leave me." I kissed her cheek and her voice in my head whispered back to me, "Calm down; it's not for long."

Miss U.D. Hunter, My Muse of Music at Coushatta Grade School

"Guess what, Momnee! I've got a music teacher now. I can't hardly believe it. Our class has a music teacher! She just appeared today like magic with her pitch pipe and her phonograph and it was real exciting because we got to sing and march and listen to music."

"Wait, wait—slow down a minute. I can't understand what you're saying; you're talking so fast. Let me put down my things and then I'll sit down with you and we can talk."

I must have surprised Momnee 'cause she just got home from work, and I'm not usually this excited. I didn't know I was gonna like school this much. Havin' a music teacher is fun because we're learnin' to sing notes. It's a little bit like readin', but in books you read letters and words and in music you read notes and songs.

Now, Momnee's back and I can't wait to sing her the song we learned today. She's takin' her good dress and good shoes off. "Momnee, listen to what I can sing! It's a 'good morning' song."

"Good morning, good morning, good morning.

The sun shines above us today

So we'll work while we work, and play while we play

That's the way to be happy and gay."

"Oh, Joy, that's lovely. I like having you sing to me. I usually sing songs to you, but now you can sing to me and I can be the listener. And I'm so glad you love music and that you're learning to read the notes. Some day you may want to learn to play the piano or some other musical instrument." Momnee hugged me and I felt real happy inside.

And then she sat down beside me with her cup of coffee and she said, "Now tell me about that new music teacher!"

Miss U.D. Hunter just appeared in our class like magic and she had a wire-and-chalk thing to make music lines and spaces on the blackboard and some other stuff that I can't remember.

She played music on her phonograph and let us march around the room even when the boys kept turnin' over the red chairs in the reading circle and got really, really noisy. I could tell right away that I was gonna LOVE music.

Miss Hunter is different from our other teachers in some ways. For one thing, she rides a bicycle to school and everywhere. It's a patriotic thing to do, with our country being in a war, but she did it even before we got in the war. I remember one day the teachers marched us all out to the big steps in front of the school where the tall columns go all the way to the top of the HUGE front porch. We all sat down on the steps and listened to speeches on the radio about the war starting. And right there by the steps, there was Miss Hunter's bicycle and they had to move it for some of us to sit down. That's how I remember how long she's been riding her bicycle.

Miss Hunter is not exactly what you'd call pretty because her teeth stick out a little bit in front—just the top row—but she has pretty black hair and wears nice clothes and has a good figure, if you know what I mean. Her legs are even prettier than Betty Grable's. She's what you'd prob'ly call attractive instead of pretty.

All the Baptists call her "Miss U.D." and the rest of us just call her Miss Hunter. She plays the piano and teaches Sunbeams and BYPU and some other stuff at the Baptist Church. One of my Baptist friends told me they call her Miss U.D. because she is ashamed to be called by her real name which is Uriah Dora. Now I didn't really believe all that because who in their right mind would name their own little baby girl a name like Uriah? But on the other hand, you never know. Miss Hunter and all her family are very religious. Maybe Uriah is a Bible name or a Baptist name but just not a very pretty one.

I asked about Miss Hunter's name one night at home when we were eating supper and my daddy told me that believe it or not, my friend was right! Here is how he explained it to me. Miss Hunter's daddy has the U.H. Hunter Dry Goods Store across the railroad tracks. His real name is Uriah Hogan Hunter and they call him Mr. U. H. Her brother is named for his daddy and they call him Hogan Junior. Her mama's name is Miss Dora so they named their daughter Uriah Dora. I thought it was too bad they couldn't of just called her Dora Junior, like her brother was called Hogan Junior, but Daddy said, "Well, those Hunters are kind of a dangerous race of people."

Then Momnee jumped into the discussion and said,

"Oh, Bob, that's not a very nice thing to say about a teacher, especially in front of these children," which ended that conversation. I really wish he could of explained what he meant, but I didn't dare ask 'cause I was scared he might get mad and start on one of his temper tantrums.

When I found out the reason for her name I decided to call Miss Hunter "Miss U.D." even if I'm not a Baptist. And anyway, I've always had a lot of Baptist friends, so I've also had a good many Baptist experiences. We're Methodists, but most of my friends are Baptists and Momnee lets me go to church things with my Baptist friends when they invite me.

The only real painful thing about having Miss U.D. for a teacher (she doesn't give us tests or grades in Music)—but she does bring her violin to school sometimes, and plays it for us. I'm glad she doesn't sing while she plays 'cause that might make it even worse. But I bet she could do it if she wanted to. I mean, if she can ride her bicycle and hold onto that big violin case at the same time, well, I figure she could play and sing at the same time if she wanted to.

I think the reason she doesn't sing is because she just loves to listen to the music she's playing. I can tell, because she closes her eyes and gets the sweetest little faraway look on her face, like maybe the angels are singing to her. But it is a bad mistake for her to close her eyes, because when she does, the boys and even some of the girls put their hands over their ears and make terrible faces. Sometimes they even make rude noises but she doesn't hear us—I mean them—giggling.

One day she was playing a church hymn for us and she came to a real high note and it got real squawky and then one of the strings broke. We thought maybe that would end it all; that maybe she wouldn't be able to play for us anymore. Some people who weren't quite music lovers yet were prob'ly kind of relieved. They prob'ly thought the whole ordeal was over, but not me. I think it's kind of fun and exciting to hear her play. You never know what might happen.

As it turned out, all she had to do was get another string from home. She probably has dozens there just waiting for her to bust another string, so those rude boys might as well just relax and try to enjoy the music. I actually look forward to the days when she brings her violin.

I think maybe even music that's not so good is better

Illustration by Ellen Gaddis Howell

than no music at all. Anyhow, I do LOVE music and I know I always will. I'm even learning to play the piano now and my piano teacher is Mrs. Edwina Stephens; but it all began in the first grade with Miss U.D.

My Friend, Robbie
Coushatta Grade School 1938

I have a new friend now, and this is one of the most exciting things that's ever happened in my life. Most of my friends live in my neighborhood, or at least go to Coushatta Grade School like I do, but not Robbie. Her real name is Robbie Sue Adams and she's been going to Coushatta High School ever since she started to school in the first grade. She's in the third grade now, just like me, but she's been going to a different school because in Coushatta, if you live on the side of the railroad tracks where the courthouse is you're sposeta go to the High School all the way from first grade till you graduate, but if you live on the side where the river bridge is, like I do you're sposeta go from the first grade to the seventh grade at the Grade School and then you get to go to the High School till you graduate. I know all that is kind of confusing, but that's why Robbie and I never did get to be in school together until now; because we lived on different sides of the railroad tracks. Here is what happened on the first day of school just last week:

Me and some of my friends at school are sitting in the middle of a little patch of grass in front of the school building close to where the ground is real hard; a place where some of the boys play marbles and the girls mostly play hopscotch. I happen to look up and see a girl that I know who hasn't been going to this school before. I remember her though and I'm real glad to see her because I played with her at her grandmother's house and we had a good time playing together.

"Hi! You must be the new girl Nellie Ruth told me about. Your name's Robbie, isn't it?" I ask, as I walk right up to this girl who's about the same size as me, only she's a lot prettier and she has curly reddish blond hair; the kind I wish I had. She looks surprised, but she's kinda smiling when she says, "Well, yes, I am new at this school, but I guess I'm really not that much newer than you are, cause we're about the same size." And then she laughs out loud and I remember that I like her a lot because she knows how to make a joke. I'll bet she even reads the funny papers like I do.

We sit down on the grass with our legs crossed in front of us, and she tells me her name and where she lives and stuff like that. It's first recess now and we're sitting here waiting for the bell to ring. Then I tell her that I remember playing with her once at her grandmother's house. Her Grandmother is "Miss Sally" Adams, who lives in the same neighborhood with me; and then she says she remembers me too, from that day at her grandmother's house. It turns out that our families are a lot alike and we like a lot of the same things and then, before I can find out anything else, the bell rings and it's time for us to go in for real school. I'm so glad we're going to be in the same class, and I hope we'll get to play together after school sometimes, too. Maybe she can come to my house, or we'll get to play together again at her grandmother's house. Her grandmother makes good tea cakes. I think Robbie and I are gonna be <u>real</u> good friends.

The 1938 Coushatta Grade School May Fete

My love/hate relationship with the Coushatta Grade School May Fete began when I was in Miss Tipton's fourth grade in the spring of 1938. I loved Miss Tipton and I loved school; it was a happy year, and then this May Fete event came into my life. This is the way I remember it:

"Boys and girls, it's time to put your Spellers away and get ready for something different and exciting. How many of you remember the May Fete from last spring? Raise your hands if you remember the big program we had in May of last year." Hands go up all over the room except for two boys'.

"James and Freddie, I forgot that you boys weren't in this school last year; of course you don't remember. Would any of the rest of you like to tell something you remember about the May Fete? Would anybody like to tell about your favorite part?"

(No hands up this time not even mine. I just hate it when I can't answer my teacher's questions.) I can't remember all that much about the May Fete except that I wore a daisy costume and sang a song about daisies with some other girls. But I don't think anybody in this class wants to hear about that.

Miss Tipton pulls out some slips of paper and lays them down on top of her desk. Everyone gets very still and quiet. ("Oh, no, I'm thinking; she's gonna give us a pop test.") Then she says, "Nobody seems to want to talk, so I'll remind you of what it's all about, and then we'll get to the interesting part; the part we're going to do today. Now listen carefully:"

"The May Day celebration that we call The May Fete reminds us that springtime is here and summer is coming soon. It's all about flowers and songs and happiness and it involves a sort of game where boys and girls wrap long colored ribbon streamers around the 'May Pole.' It's hard to describe, but you'll get to see it soon enough as we begin to prepare for the program. On a night near May 1st a stage will be set up and your parents and everybody in the community will be invited to come and see it."

"What we need to do today is elect one of the girls to represent our class in the contest to be May Queen. We do this by voting, since our country is a democracy; we choose our leaders by voting, you know. That's what these sheets of paper are for. They are your ballots; you need to find the name of the girl you want to be Queen of the fourth grade, and put a check by her name." She holds one of the papers up for us to see and then she makes a big check on the blackboard. "You only get one vote, so think carefully about who you want to represent us as Queen."

As the papers are being passed from front to back on each row, my heart beats faster, because I hardly ever have to make important decisions like this. I have lots of girl friends and I don't know who will be the best one; should I vote for the prettiest, or the smartest, or the friendliest, or the nicest? I guess it wouldn't be right to say, "eeny, meeny, miney, mo,'" on something important like this.

(Oh, no. She's coming to take up our ballads. I thought ballads were songs?)

She asks one of the boys to come up and help her with the counting. Miss Tipton asks him to announce the winner. When he says, "The winner is Edith Joy," I'm so shocked I nearly fall out of my chair. I raise my hand real quick, and when Miss Tipton calls on me I say, "I think maybe y'all need to count the votes over again; there must be some mistake." She looks at me kind of funny and asks," Why do you say that?"

"Well," I answer, "whenever we choose up sides for ball games and races and things I'm almost always the last one chosen, so this has got to be a mistake." They count over again and it's still me.

Miss Tipton sort of chuckles and says, "Edith Joy, you're not one of the best runners or ball players in the class, but you do well with a lot of other things, like helping other people, so maybe that's why you were chosen this time."

Well! That was exciting. Now it's time to go out for PE, and I can go back to being the last one chosen, for whatever we're playing today.

Royalty Pains

"Momnee, Momnee! Guess what happened today! I haven't been this excited since I got to be an angel in the Christmas pageant in first grade. You can never guess, because I thought it was a mistake at first. I thought Miss Tipton must have made a mistake counting the votes, but she didn't, and I got elected to be May Queen of the fourth grade. I'm not queen of the whole school, of course; just the fourth grade, but it's still a good thing to be."

Momnee looks surprised, but now that she's over the surprise I can tell she's happy, and she hugs me real tight. "That's just wonderful, Joy. I'm so proud of you. It's quite an honor to be chosen by your classmates to be their Queen of the May Fete. They must really think you're a nice person. Now you need to live up to that by remembering to be nice to everyone. Sometimes that's hard to do, especially if someone is not nice to you, but I know you can do it."

"Momnee, I don't think that'll be too hard, because most people like me okay. But part of this May Queen business is going to be really, really hard. I hope you won't mind about this, but I'm gonna hafta have a queen dress. Can Miss Evie sew it for us? I know you don't have time to sew, because you work at your office all the time, and it has to be made by a special pattern and out of a certain kind of material from L.P. Stephens Store."

"And there's another thing I may need your help with. It's about choosing a king. Miss Tipton told me how it works: each grade elects their queen and then each of these queens has to choose the king for that grade. I really don't like that part, because my two very best friends are Bert Stephens and Keete Lockett Hester and I think I like them both about the same, so I'm afraid whichever one I don't choose will get his feelings hurt and never like me anymore. What am I gonna do? I'm not sure I even want to be queen at all if it has to be like that. I don't think children my age should have to make hard decisions like this, do you? Can queens resign?"

Momnee kind of smiles, and says, "Well, if it will help your feelings any, I can tell you this: You don't need to worry about the queen dress. I can handle that part. As for choosing the king, I'm sorry – that's your problem. I wish I could help you, but only you can make that choice. I think they're both very nice boys. I know they're both good friends of yours. Good luck! I know you can handle it."

There's another problem I'm thinking about, but I'm not even telling Momnee about it yet. I've been wondering about some other things I don't quite understand about the May Fete. Daddy's just walking in the door now. Maybe I'll ask Daddy about it if he seems to be in a good mood.

"Daddy, I just got elected fourth grade queen for the May Fete today." (I've got my fingers crossed hoping he'll be proud of me like Momnee is.) He looks even more surprised than Momnee did and he is smiling so I know that's a good sign.

"Well, well," he says. "Your classmates must really like you and think you're a good leader. I just hope you won't think you can run things here at home, though, now that you're a queen." I can tell he's just teasing me now, so I'll try asking him about my other problem.

"Oh, no, Daddy. I know I'm not even queen of the whole school. You see, this is the way it works: Every grade elects their own queen, and then we all try to get our parents and friends and everybody we know to vote for our queen by giving one penny for every vote, so our grade's queen will be the real Queen of May for the whole school and for the May Fete this year. I'm also s'posed to tell you that the money we collect will be used to buy educational stuff that the school needs. I have a letter for you from the principal, but Daddy, there's something I don't understand. If we're a democracy why do people have to pay money to vote? What does money have to do with voting?"

"Everything!" Daddy laughs as he reaches in his pocket, pulls out a dollar bill and hands it to me. You'll understand this kinda stuff better when you're a little older. For right now, let's just say it's a donation to a good cause and leave it at that."

"Gosh, thanks, Daddy. That's a hundred votes for me!" By now, I'm skipping off to find some of my neighborhood friends to tell about this. I hope they'll be as easy to convince as Daddy was and I'm sure glad he was in such a good humor. But I still wonder about the whole thing about money and voting. Oh, well, as Aunt Howard says, "I ask too many questions" and maybe she's right.

Now I guess it's time to start worrying about the king problem again. Right now I'm kinda leaning toward choosing Keete Lockett. He lives almost in my neighborhood only closer to the bridge, and sometimes we skate to school together. We really have more in common 'cause he has red hair and freckles like me, and he says funny things sometimes. But Bert is real nice, too. He takes piano lessons and has an accordion that he's learning to play. His family has a lot of money, but I don't think you should vote for a person just because of that. He's not snobby at all, but I really think he wants to be king. I think either one of them would make a good king. This is a hard decision.

The time finally comes when I have to make my

decision. Today! It turns out to be a little easier than I thought it would be. I know I have to choose Keete Lockett. Bert comes to school today bringing me a big box of candy which is really nice for me, but I decide it just wouldn't be fair to choose him just because of that; that would be making my decision for selfish reasons. I guess maybe I should have told him I couldn't take the gift, but I did share the candy with other people and it sure was good. I'm glad that's over with, and I prob'ly made an unwise choice, but it was a fair one, and I like for things to be fair. I just hope Bert will keep on being my friend. He probably will because I know he really likes me and Keete Lockett, and he likes for things to be fair, too.

Well, all this May Queen stuff is just about over, and I'm sure glad. For one thing, I don't really like going around asking people for money, even if it's for a good cause. Another thing is, now that I've gotten involved in all this, I hope I won't be too disappointed if I don't win. When the voting is all over, all the kings and queens who don't win will get demoted down to being just dukes and duchesses, but they still get to march in the parade and wear their royal costumes. The only difference is, the REAL King and Queen of the May Fete get to wear crowns in the pageant and carry scepters which are just sticks covered with glittery stuff—but they're not magic or anything. So who cares?

We found out today that the second grade queen and king won the contest and they'll get to be the REAL king and queen for the whole school for this year's May Fete. Can you believe those little second-graders collected nearly twice as much money as we fourth-graders did?

The May Fete continued for decades. In 1962 Bob Gaddis as King, Blanche Gaddis as his page, Suzanne Bethard as Queen.

I'm a little bit disappointed, but Betty Jo, as little as she is, will prob'ly be a much better May Queen in some ways than me. She has long brown hair and no freckles at all. And now maybe Bert won't be mad at me, because I don't think he'd like being a duke nearly as much as being a king. Maybe this whole business has a happy ending after all.

White Collar Crime in Miss Tressie's Fifth Grade

If you ruin your good reputation at a young age I wonder if you can ever get it back again. I sure hope so. It's a lot easier on kids if they have a good reputation with teachers. It really doesn't matter that much what other kids think about you because they forget, but you can ruin your reputation with teachers so fast it's amazing and it feels just terrible when it happens. Sometimes I can't believe I did something that bad; that we all did. I'm usually too scared to ever take chances about doing dangerous things. It's not that I'm really all that good about going by the rules and all that; I'm just not brave enough to take a lot of chances. I know I'm not a brave person especially when it comes to making grown-ups mad; especially teachers; and *Daddy*. Yep, he's the main one I don't want to make mad; if he ever finds out about what I did he prob'ly won't ever forgive me. I really hope *God* will forgive me, because I sure don't want to get in trouble with God this early in my life. Why, oh why did I do it?

But when it comes to doing *stupid* things, well sometimes it's almost like I left my brain at home. I should have known we'd get caught. But it just seemed like such a good opportunity. I don't even remember whose idea it was, but maybe it was Ira Jr.'s, because he's real smart and everybody loved the idea because it sounded like an adventure. I thought it seemed like something that Nancy Drew might do in one of her mystery books; besides, having a secret is always fun.

So this is how it all happened: There were six of us fifth-graders and six of the sixth-graders who had been selected by the teachers to run off tests (for the other class, of course) on the hectograph machine. It was really fun because we got to be out of the classroom and I guess it kind of meant we were "teachers' pets" but not really. It was just that our teachers trusted us because we made good grades and didn't need to cheat. Or was it maybe that the teachers thought we were too dumb to think of such a plan? Fifth-graders swapping with sixth-graders? Come to think of it, that's a lot of people to keep a secret, isn't it? No, I think they trusted us.

Well, anyway that's what we did and at first it was fun, swapping the tests at recess. Doing exciting things like that can make you feel good at first, but then all of a sudden you get all sweaty and scared and shaky inside and just a little bit sickish. I didn't expect it to be quite like that. I wondered and wondered. "Where could I hide my stolen test so no one would see? It wasn't really stolen was it? I know it's wrong to steal. I guess it's wrong to cheat, too, but is cheating as bad as stealing?" And then, suddenly I figured out what to do.

Momnee's office (the Welfare Office) was right across the street from the school. Lots of days I would walk over to her office on my way home from school and say hello to her. That office used to be somebody's house and there was an old wooden icebox under the carport just as you went in the side door. So I figured that I could put that old test that was beginning to drive me crazy in there and never look at it again. I never even used it but I sure didn't forget about it.

I thought I could forget, but I was wrong. The more I tried to forget about it the more I thought about that test. The more I told myself this hadn't really happened the more sweaty and shaky I got so it was almost a relief when two days later all twelve of us were called before Miss Tressie Cooper's "supreme court." I was so ashamed I didn't even stop to wonder how they found out.

I will always remember that as one of the worst days of my life. We had to stand up in a line in front of all the fifth and sixth-graders, not to mention Miss Tressie and Mr. Bobbitt, the Principal. It was awful. I just remember the teachers saying how disappointed they were in us. And you could tell they really meant it because of the religious looks on their faces. The rest of what they said sounded a lot like a sermon, and by that time our heads were down, and most of us were probably praying because we kind of guessed that God was pretty upset with us, too and was not likely to be on our side when the bad news got to our parents. Even though we had made the choice to become criminals at such a young age we knew that our parents—Methodists, Baptists, or whatever church they went to—were all on the side of the Lord when it came to sinning and stuff like that. And they all knew that old "spare the rod" scripture verse from the Bible. We got preached to that day and it was sort of like church only without the hymns.

Of course the teachers had already let us know whose side they were on and the girls (us guilty ones) were all crying; I guess to prove we were really truly sorry. It was a terrible mess. One girl wet her pants and made a little puddle on the floor, but it wasn't me; I guess I shouldn't even mention that incident. Maybe the reason we all took it so hard was that we were s'posed to be the good kids and now, Lord knows if we would ever be trusted with anything again at that school or at home. It really was just awful. But we did truly repent and none of the girls got whipped but the boys did and some of them didn't even cry. Prob'ly everybody got whipped again at home; that's what parents called an unwritten rule back in those days.

It's strange but most of the really bad things in my life

Illustration by Ellen Gaddis Howell

have taught me a lesson. There's prob'ly something in the Bible about that. There's a hymn we sing a lot in church that says "Are there trials and temptations? Is there trouble anywhere?" I found out the temptations come first and then the trials, and then, it seems like there's trouble everywhere. And this time I learned two things: One thing is I will never cheat in school again even if I need to, and I hope I never need to but I probably will. The other thing is that it's prob'ly a good idea to skip some of the wonderful opportunities that come along even if they sound like fun.

CHAPTER 5

Real Life Lessons

Hometown Religion

I WONDER ABOUT a lot of things that grown-ups talk about sometimes; specially when they don't know I'm listening. I guess maybe I shouldn't be listening, and that's why I don't ask about those things because I know it's not polite to listen to grown people's conversations when they're not talking to you, but I can't help wondering. I'd ask Momnee, because I'm sure she'd know a lot of the answers but she has to work all day at her office or out in the field, which is when she visits clients in their homes. Then when she comes home she has to see about us kids and read us stories and get us ready for bed. Sometimes I can tell she's real tired because she goes to sleep when she reads to us.

Anyway, Momnee knows a lot about religion and she talks to us children about God and Jesus when she reads us stories from the Bible. I think some of the things I keep wondering about are about religion, but I'm not sure. Now that I can read pretty good I prob'ly need to read the Bible myself. I hate to admit this because it's prob'ly a bad sin, but I don't enjoy reading the Bible very much. Some of the words are so hard; I know how to pronounce 'em from hearing them in church but they're kind of confusing and I just don't get it. Momnee says that's because it's written in King James English, like people used to talk a long, long time ago. It seems like I understand it a lot better when Momnee reads it to me but sometimes I just go to sleep. That's prob'ly a sin, too.

I guess religion is mostly about church but I have a feeling there's a lot more to it than that. I'm not saying that church isn't important but what I think is that religion is more about God than it is about church. Another thing I don't understand is why we have so many different religions and most of the people in them are Christians, but some of them are called Baptists and some Methodists and Catholics and Presbyterians and that's not even including Jews and Hindus and lots of other kinds.

I learned the Apostles' Creed when I was real little and I say it every Sunday in church but I still don't understand a lot of the stuff in it even though I'm ten now. So I say I believe in a lot of things I don't really understand but I figured out for myself that it's okay to do that because prob'ly someday I will understand them and believe in them. I know I believe in God; I'm not real sure why but I think it's because Momnee does and I want to be like her. As far as Jesus Christ his only son our Lord, and the Holy Spirit and the Virgin Mary and Pontius Pilate, well, I think I'll just have to wait until I get all that straightened out. Momnee explained to me about the holy catholic church and it doesn't mean you have to be a Catholic to be a Christian. That just means the church is all over the world. I looked it up and catholic means universal. I think God made the whole universe and that's just about everything.

Here in Coushatta about all we have is Methodists and Baptists, but there are worlds of them; especially Baptists. There used to be some Jewish families in town, but there's only two of them still living here now and they're real nice. One family is the Lissos and they have a daughter who is a little older than me and she comes to our Sunday School sometimes. The other family is the Bernsteins and I like to go to their store to buy candy.

It must be a lot harder being a Baptist than being a Methodist. I've never actually been a Baptist but I have had a lot of Baptist experiences because one of our friends is Joyce Ann Cheatham, the Baptist preacher's daughter. I've gone with her to Sunbeams and GA's after school and they have to learn a lot of Bible verses. If they say them right they get prizes and certificates and things. I think they're more afraid of forgetting those verses than forgetting to do their homework. If you ask me, Methodists get off pretty light about stuff like that. We read the Bible a lot in church but we hardly ever have to memorize verses and say 'em in front of people. Just at Christmas and Easter and only if you really want to at Sunday School.

I like everything about the Baptist Church just fine except for the religious part. I'm talking about things like getting baptized. I'm glad I got baptized when I was too little to remember it. I have a great fear of drowning and if I had to do it the Baptist way I'm afraid I might scream and struggle and that would prob'ly ruin the whole thing. Methodists, even the little tiny babies, could never drown from that little bit of water on their heads, and the pastor holding them. You have to be brave to be a Baptist.

One thing I really like is that Baptists have such good refreshments at their parties and church meetings. You know how they always serve tuna salad sandwiches at church things? Well, my friends argue a lot about which is best, Methodist or Baptist tuna but I like both. In fact I almost can't tell the difference.

I've been to lots of revivals at the Baptist Church because I go to the Coushatta Grade School. My school is only a block from the Baptist Church. When they have their revivals our teachers line us up and march us to the church for the morning preaching services. We all sit together, row after row after row of us and we are always real quiet because there are a lot of Baptist teachers at our school. Especially Miss U.D. Hunter. She's our music teacher and she knows all the Baptist hymns and she can play them on the piano and her violin.

The first and second graders have to stay at school instead of going to the revivals because they're prob'ly not old enough to get saved. I'm always afraid I might get saved and have to walk down to the front and I'm not sure if it's okay for Methodists to get saved at the Baptist Church. I probably could just rededicate my life but I'm not sure exactly what that means so when they have an invitation to come down front I always just hold on tight to the seat and try to stay right where I am.

I've been invited to go to Baptist camp this summer with Joyce Ann and her family only they call it Encampment and the boys and girls can't go swimming together. I'm kind of wondering about that; I hope it doesn't mean they swim without suits on. I'm afraid to ask Joyce Ann about it so I'll just take my chances on it. After all, Methodists and Baptists can't be that different, can they? I'm really excited about going to that encampment; it's way down in south Louisiana at a place called Mandeville, and it's on Lake Pontchartrain, which is a big, big lake.

One time my little sister Alexa and I went to have Sunday dinner at the Cheathams' house. (Baptists call their preacher's house a parsonage just like Methodists do.) Their parsonage is pretty fancy and I was afraid one of us might do or say something embarrassing but we did just fine. Momnee teaches us a lot about manners, and I think it must be pretty important to get things like that right. It's a big responsibility having a little sister. She's real smart but sometimes she just thinks about things too much. If you ask me, I think we'd be better off not to think too much about things, especially religious stuff; it can be scary sometimes.

Just to give you an example, When Alexa was real little she used to think that Mr. Ed Holley, our Sunday School Superintendent, was God because every Sunday he got up in front of the assembly and told how many people were at Sunday School and how much the offering was and things like that. I tried to explain to her the difference between God and the Sunday School Super-intendent but I could tell she didn't believe me. For a long time I worried that she might see him downtown or somewhere and run up to him and say "Hello, God." That would be embarrassing. Thank goodness she never did do anything like that, and now she's old enough to know better.

The Cheathams have a nice dining room and a cook to make the dinner and serve it. Mrs. Cheatham has a little bell on the table that goes "ping" when she punches it and the cook comes right out of the kitchen like magic. I didn't know about the bell until she pinged it so I almost turned over my water glass. That would have been an embarrassing fox pass. (New word I learned in a Movie magazine. It's spelled f-a-u-x p-a-s. I love new words.)

Bessie the cook looked nice in her white ruffly apron and cap. "That was a good meal, Bessie," Mrs. Cheatham said. "Chicken just a tad on the dry side but we'll work on that. We're ready for dessert and coffee now."

Bessie made a quick little bow. I think she meant it to be a curtsy like the little princesses Elizabeth and Margaret Rose make before the queen in the news reels, but Bessie must of weighed at least 200 pounds and that would of been hard for her to do.

"Oh, and Bessie, fix yourself a plate now and you can go on home as soon as you finish cleaning up," Mrs. Cheatham said; she has the prettiest smile. She's real nice and she serves Sunday dinner a little more formally than we do at our house.

After dinner Joyce Ann asked if we could go to the picture show. Mrs Cheatham got a serious look on her face and said, "No, Joyce Ann, you know we don't go to the moving pictures on Sunday."

Well, Joyce Ann really wanted to go—it was a Mickey Rooney movie. He's so funny. We all wanted to go. Alexa and I even had our dimes ready for the tickets. I knew

Momnee would of let us go if this was happening at our house.

"Mother, why can't we go? What's so wrong about it? It's just a picture show, and we love Mickey Rooney. Besides, everybody else is going."

"Joyce Ann, you're not allowed to go to the show on Sunday and that's that." Mrs. Cheatham was about to run out of patience. I was hoping good ole Joyce Ann wouldn't ask again. But she just wouldn't give up on it.

"It's just not a Christian thing to do dear, because if you go to the show that means that others will have to work on Sunday selling tickets, making popcorn and running the film. And if the preacher's daughter is allowed to go it would set a bad example."

Well, that did make perfect sense to me but I could tell my little sister did not understand. She had that look on her face. She was thinking again. And worrying. Later when we were walking home she said, "Joy, if Mrs. Cheatham is right about all that Sabbath Day stuff then why does she make Bessie cook and clean up on Sunday? That's working, isn't it?"

You see what I mean about Alexa? She worries a lot for a child. Since I'm almost two years older than her I do my best to help her stay on the right track but sometimes it's hard. I do try though, because I don't want her waking me up at night with her worries. So I say in my best calm, adult voice, "Well there are some mysteries in God's world that we're just not old enough to understand; or maybe you have to be a Baptist."

That night when I tried to go to sleep I thought about Bessie and I wondered if Alexa was still worrying about that situation. I looked over at her head on the pillow next to mine. She was sound asleep.

Chocolate Fudge with a Little Crunch

I really like for my friend, Dorothy, to come over to play, but that doesn't happen very often because she lives a long way off in another town. I only get to see her when she comes to visit her aunt and uncle who live in Coushatta. Her uncle, Reverend Staples, is pastor of the Methodist Church here. The parsonage where he lives is not far from our neighborhood so when she comes to visit him and his wife they let her come over to play with me. We were playing "Monopoly" one afternoon, which, as everybody knows, takes a long time to play and we were getting a little bit bored. Then I got a sudden inspiration.

"Do you like to cook, Dorothy?" I asked, hoping she was as ready for a change as I was. "I've never done much cooking," she answered, "but I wouldn't mind learning," she added with a smile.

"Oh good!" I exclaimed, eager to show off my cooking skills. This seemed like a good afternoon to make chocolate fudge. I ran to get the recipe, the one on the Hershey's Cocoa box, and the ingredients for the fudge. I enjoyed playing with Dorothy. She was real easy to get along with and pretty as well, with dark, almost black hair and pretty skin with NO freckles.

"I think this bowl will be a good one for mixing and this white pan to cook it in," I said, selecting a crockery bowl and a white enamelware saucepan. I really didn't have much experience with cooking, because Aunt Howard looks after us kids when Momnee is at her office working and she doesn't have much patience with kids in the kitchen. But what I lacked in experience I made up for in confidence and enthusiasm. I loved chocolate fudge, and I had helped make it a few times.

The saucepan I selected had a chipped place in the bottom but I didn't think that would matter. It was much prettier than the one Momnee usually used. I had never seen her use this one. Maybe she only used it for company but of course Dorothy was company; especially since she was from out of town. I was sure I had made a good choice.

We dumped the ingredients into the bowl, poured the whole thing into the saucepan, lit the gas burner on the stove and began stirring with all our might, taking turns when we got tired. A little bit sloshed out on the stove and the linoleum floor, but we didn't worry about that. We told ourselves that we would clean it all up later when we put away the cocoa, sugar, butter, milk and vanilla. And we would wash all the bowls and measuring cups, too. We didn't want to make any extra work for Aunt Howard; she gets real nervous and upset when we make big messes, especially in the kitchen.

"When will the fudge be ready?" asked Dorothy. "This is fun but I'm getting a little tired, and hungry too, aren't you?"

"Yes, I really am but we have to be sure it's done or it won't get hard," I answered, with more confidence than I was feeling now. "If it doesn't get hard it will be all runny and we'll have to eat it with a spoon and it's not very good that way." I was beginning to worry about this whole undertaking but I couldn't let Dorothy know. So we stirred more vigorously. Soon I began to feel a little crunch in the bottom of the pan. I was sure that this meant that the fudge was done.

"We can turn the fire off now and put the pan in a dishpan of cold water to cool it off. After it cools we have to beat it and beat it until it starts getting hard. Then we pour it on a platter until it gets really hard and then we can cut it into little squares. Oh! I almost forgot; we need to butter the platter while we're waiting for the fudge to cool. Here, I'll show you how to do that," I said to Dorothy. This was beginning to seem like a lot of work to me. I was losing my enthusiasm for this project and my appetite for fudge along with it. I could tell by the look on Dorothy's face that she was feeling the same way I did.

At that very moment Fred Jr. came bursting in, banging the screen door and yelling, "I smell fudge. It sure smells good." I never could figure out how he could smell fudge from way across the street at his house but he always did. He never failed to show up when we made fudge. And then a little smile flickered across my face. In a twinkling I had figured out who was going to beat the fudge. Sure 'nuf, he was glad to do it. We were glad too, even though he did lick the spoon a time or two even when I reminded him not to.

Once the fudge was cut into squares it looked yummy and it had a wonderful smell. Our appetites began to return and we couldn't wait to bite into it. Fred Jr. grabbed the first piece.

"Well, how is it, we asked?" We were both feeling that

momentary anxiety that most cooks feel when the first person takes a taste of their latest creation.

"It's REAL good," Fred Jr. answered, grabbing another piece. "You must of put nuts in it. It has a little crunch to it," and he stuffed another piece in his mouth.

Watching Fred Jr. eat caused Dorothy and me to recover our appetites and we dug in, too. At that moment Aunt Howard appeared in the doorway. Her face turned red as a beet as soon as she looked around at the mess in the kitchen. Pots and pans and dribbles of chocolate were everywhere, not to mention the box of cocoa that Fred Jr. had managed to turn over while beating the fudge a little too energetically.

"Lordy mercy!" Aunt Howard wailed with her hands in the air. "I can't leave you kids by yourselves for a minute. I had everything cleaned up and now you couldn't find Jesus if he was here in this kitchen." She flung her arms about, shaking a finger at all the mess to emphasize her point.

We didn't know what to do now. We certainly couldn't plead innocence. The evidence was all around us. I decided that penitence was our only alternative.

"I'm so sorry, Aunt Howard; I know I should have asked before I did something like this. We didn't mean to do anything wrong. We'll clean it all up, I promise!" I was pleading for mercy with my eyes as well as my words. We might never get to cook again!

"You're mighty right you'll clean it up and without any help from me," she blurted out. Noting her scowl, I rethought the problem. Maybe lying and bribery would be more effective than throwing ourselves on her mercy in this situation.

"I'm so sorry, Aunt Howard. I thought it would be a nice surprise for you. You must be real tired from washing the clothes. Why don't you sit down and rest and we'll bring you some fudge; and a glass of water, too; you must be thirsty from being out there washing clothes." She was beginning to soften; I could see a tiny glimmer of a smile on her face. She had little crinkles around her eyes when she smiled. I was hoping she didn't suspect my deceit.

"That candy does smell good," she said as she dropped herself into a chair, propped up her feet and waited to be served. I breathed a sigh of relief as she bit into the fudge, but then she got a strange expression on her face. She took one more bite and her eyes widened.

"What did y'all put in this candy?" she wanted to know. By that time she was out of her chair and hurrying back toward the kitchen.

"Oh, just the usual stuff. We used the recipe on the cocoa box. You know, cocoa, sugar, vanilla…" She cut me off. "What did you COOK it in?" Then she spied the white enamel saucepan and her arms flew up in the air again. "Oh, Lordy mercy, Lordy mercy! Did all of you eat the fudge?" As we nodded yes, she began wringing her hands.

Without another word she went straight to the telephone. We heard her ask the operator to ring Dr. Davis' number. I heard her say the word "emergency" and then I heard her tell Dr. Davis that his own grandson was involved in this escapade. Then I heard her say, "I'm TRYING to calm down but these children may be dying right now. Those chips of enamel are just like pieces of glass." I didn't hear the other side of the conversation, of course, but later I found out it went something like this:

"Now Howard, don't get all het up. Those young'uns are gonna be all right. Just feed 'em as much light bread as you can get 'em to choke down. No, don't put anything on it, just plain light bread. And you don't need to worry about any of 'em dyin'. If they're all as hard headed as my grandson, Fred Jr., well, neither the Lord nor the devil wants 'em. If you see any blood just let me know."

Looking Back, Post Retirement

Thinking back recently to this episode that happened so many years ago, I became more and more caught up in the past. I could smell the fudge, hear Aunt Howard's panicked voice as she talked on the phone to Dr. Davis. I remembered the relief of all the parties involved when this story turned out to have an uneventful ending.

No one had to go to the hospital; no one even got sick. We were the talk of the neighborhood for a few days but no real harm was done. In fact, we got off light considering what we had done. We didn't have to endure a visit from Dr. Davis with his big booming voice and presence and we didn't even have to clean up the kitchen because everyone was so worried and so busy getting that light bread down us.

However, we did have to face the possibility of our own mortality at a tender age and I had to wrestle with my conscience for a long time afterward. I knew that lying and deceit were wrong, were in fact sins; but I didn't have the courage to face Aunt Howard with a full confession. I still had a lot to learn, the hard way; but that would be another story or two.

Loreco Café

When Daddy bought the Loreco Café and Service Station it changed the lives of the family living in the "little house" on Twitchell Street quite a bit. A whole new world of responsibilities was slung onto the shoulders of the adults who lived and worked there. It became Momnee's responsibility to plan and purchase groceries for the noon meals and pies to be sold from the café lunch counter, in addition to her duties as housewife, mother and Welfare Office Worker. Aunt Howard's main duties were still childcare and housekeeping tasks but she was now also needed to help with the cooking and kitchen clean-up involved in preparing all that food at the "little house" to be served at the café.

Not only did the work load multiply for the adults in the family but the size and complexity of the household changed as well with the addition of several new members to the group we referred to as "the help." Mary Jones, a capable young black woman, was hired to cook the food to be served at the café as "plate lunches" and pies. A man called Shorty and Mary's husband, Melvin, worked at the service station as well as the café and were now responsible for transporting the meals from home to café and any other heavy work at the house which the women couldn't handle, including emergency runs to the grocery store. Everybody seemed to take all this change in stride. I never heard anyone complain. I guess they didn't have time for complaining; during the Depression people were just glad to have work to do and the pay that went with it.

If we kids had any responsibilities they were for us to "stay out of the kitchen", to "play out of doors" as much as possible, to "come when called," and by all means, to "stay out of trouble!" That kitchen in the "Little House" was probably the busiest place in the town of Coushatta during the morning hours of any week-day in the late 1930's and early '40's. From 11:00 am until 1:00 pm the Loreco Café was the busiest and most crowded place in town.

Loreco Café – Coushatta's Version of "Hamburger Heaven"

It's lunchtime now and Lexa and I are on our way from the Coushatta Grade School to our favorite eating place, the Loreco Café. Ever since Daddy bought the café, Lexa and I quit walking home from school every day for our lunch; now we walk the two blocks to the Loreco Café instead. All our friends envy us. Most of them bring their lunches to school and eat out on the playground or in the big hall. We used to be jealous of them, 'cause we had to walk home and eat ole vegetables and they got to bring peanut butter sandwiches and cookies and stuff like that. Some of 'em even have lunch boxes an' it's kinda fun, like havin' a picnic under the big oak trees in the school yard.

Sometimes if we beg real hard Momnee makes sandwiches for us and lets us take our lunch to school in a paper sack with an apple and eat with our friends. But now we like goin' to the café to eat even better. We're almost there now an' I can already smell those hamburgers cookin' on that big ole grill. I think we're real lucky that Daddy has a café.

"Hurry, Lexa," I say to my little sister. She's kinda pokey, but I guess it's hard for her to keep up with me now that I'm so much bigger than her. "Smellin' those hamburgers is makin' my mouth water; I can almost taste 'em."

"I don't know why smellin' those hamburgers makes you so hungry, Joy. It just makes me kinda sad, 'cause I know Daddy won't let us have hamburgers. We'll just have to eat those ole plate lunches an' that's just like eatin' at home. An' you *know* we can't have cokes; we'll hafta drink that ole glass o' milk jus' like we do at home."

Lexa does look sad. I wish I hadn't even brought it up. And she's right, just like she usually is. Might as well just push the thought of hamburgers out of my mind.

One time when our little sister Neenie was eatin' lunch here with us, one of the waitresses took her order, an' she said just as big as you please, " I just want a grilled cheese sandrich," and would you believe when Daddy heard that he just laughed and let her have exackly what she wanted. That kinda proves how spoiled she is.

"Oh, well, maybe Daddy'll give us a nickel when we finish our lunch and we can go to the fruit stand next door and get donuts for dessert." (I know candy is outta the question, of course, but we can get two of those good

Southern Maid Donuts for a nickel; one for Lexa and one for me.)

"Boy, this place is full o' people today, isn't it?" Lexa says just what I'm already thinkin' as we walk in the door. "Daddy must be makin' a lotta money, huh?" she asks me.

"Yeah, I sure hope so but look how hard he and Callie Bee hafta work cookin' those hamburger patties on that hot grill." I answer. "I really *am* gettin' hungry watchin' Daddy mash those patties just a little bit an' then flip 'em over. Look how he lets that grease drip back over 'em off the spatula. They smell *so good*. Almost as good as when he cooks stuff on our barbecue pit at home in the back yard."

We each sit down on a stool side by side an' then we hear, "Look out, girls, here come your lunches and they're good an' hot now, so y'all be careful," Janice smiles real big at us as she sets the plates down in front of us. "Mm, they really look good today, don't they?" She's one of the waitresses and she's real nice and friendly.

She's right about the lunches; the pork chops are browned just right and the sweet potatoes have little marshmallows on top. Mary Jones is a real good cook. I'm still sorry I can't have a hamburger but I know some of the kids in my class just have biscuits an' syrup in their lunch sacks, so it wouldn't be nice to complain at a time like this. We're so lucky.

One thing that's fun about eatin' here at the café is listenin' to the grown-ups talk. Some of 'em work at the courthouse and I like to hear about all the stuff that happens there. Sometimes it gets real exciting because it's about the court, an' the judge, an' people havin' to go to

Daddy, Louise, Neenie and Alexa at The Loreco Cafe

jail and stuff like that. My friend Robbie's daddy works at the court house in the Clerk's Office and I went with her to his office after school one day. Somebody took us up to the hangin' tower to see where they hang people but they don't do that much anymore. That was exciting, but I think my daddy's café is even more fun.

I like all of the waitresses here. They're real pretty. My favorite one is Louise Rigdon. She goes out on dates with my cousin, Rex Stothart. He goes to college in Natchitoches now, but she told me they like to go dancin' on the weekends. They go to a place called Fuzzy's. I bet one of these days they might even get married. But right now, Louise lives all by herself in a room she rents at a house here in this very same block where the café is, right across from the Baptist Church. Momnee told me that Louise was a pretty little first-grade girl in the school at Methvin when Momnee was a teacher there before she and Daddy got married.

Another one of the waitresses is Callie Bee Dickson. She's kin to Fred Jr. who lives across the street from us. But most of the time she just helps Daddy cook the hamburgers and other kinds of sandwiches and stuff like bacon and eggs. She has a husband who is gonna have to go off to the war pretty soon I think.

Momnee says some of the things I hear at the café are just gossip. She says I shouldn't be listenin' to other people's conversations anyway. But one of the things that I heard about I know is true though, and it's just awful. It's prob'ly the worst thing that ever happened in this town. There's this man and his wife and little baby daughter. They useta come in here to eat sometimes an' that little girl was so cute. She had cottony-white hair that curled all over her head like Lexa's, and she sat right up there on a stool by her mama an' daddy. But they don't come here anymore and the reason is they're dead now; all three of 'em.

What happened is that the daddy killed the whole family. It wasn't that he was mad at them or anything like that, he was just mentally ill. That's what Momnee said. But I heard some people say he was crazy. One night he killed them both with an axe when they were asleep in their beds and then he killed his mother who lived with them, too. The reason I know this is not just a story somebody made up to scare people with is that somebody came to our house in the middle of the night and got Daddy to go out and help look for the man. They found him not far from his house where he had gone and laid down on the railroad tracks until the train came along and ran over him and killed him, too. I know it was all true because everybody was talkin' about it and it was in the paper, too. Not just in the Coushatta Citizen, either. It was even in the Shreveport Times.

Sometimes when he's not too busy Daddy brings our little red-headed brother Will down to the café and lets him have an orange crush, and then Shorty, who works here, looks after him if Daddy has things to tend to. I think Daddy just likes to show Will off to his customers because he's so cute, and the only boy in the family. Will likes gettin' all that attention includin' the cold drinks, and Shorty treats him like he's somethin' special. I bet Aunt Howard likes havin' him outta her hair for a little while, too, although she just about adores him. I don't know if Daddy makes a lot of

Shorty and Will

money at the café or not, but it sure has changed the lives of the Stothart family and if you ask me it's a good thing. We have a lot more excitement than we used to.

The Power of Prayer – My View from 1941

Sometimes when I think back to my childhood I can't believe what a dumb little kid I was. I had most of my teachers fooled but that was because I was a good reader; reading sort of came natural to me and teachers seemed to like it that I read with expression. I wasn't especially good at math but they didn't seem to notice that as much. Maybe my teachers didn't like math very much either. I'm almost twelve now and there are still lots of things I don't know much about but the worst thing is, I don't really understand a lot of the things I already know.

For example, I don't know much about religion even though I've been going to Sunday school and church just about every Sunday for my whole life. Momnee read me Bible stories all the time when I was little and I read the Bible now but there's a lot of it I don't understand. For instance, in Sunday school they teach us that God is loving and merciful and that he loves us and forgives us when we're sinful but there's a lot of stuff in the Old Testament about wars and violence and killing innocent people and sometimes God seems to be okay with that. But then his own beloved son, Jesus, comes along in the New Testament and says we're supposed to love everybody, including our enemies and be nice to them even when they're mean to us. I'm telling you, it's right there in the Book of Matthew.

Then there's the part about Jesus, who never committed one sin in his whole life having to be killed because the rest of us are sinners. Tell me that's not confusing? I believe in God and I believe in Jesus Christ and I say so every Sunday morning in the Apostle's Creed, which I learned when I was real little, but I believe all that mostly because Momnee does, not because I understand what it's all about.

I remember one day when I was little, playing with my neighborhood friends, Billy and Peewee Hand, who are about my age. We were beginning to get bored playing a card game and the boys started arguing, so I said, "Hey, I have an idea! Why don't we play 'church'?"

Peewee kind of frowned up and said, "Why would we want to do that?" I could tell he wasn't very interested but I liked my idea so I had to defend it. "Well," I persisted, "we play 'school' and 'office' and 'grocery store' sometimes, so why not play 'church? Don't you like to go to church, Pewee?"

"No, not very much; and anyway, it's not even Sunday. Let's play something else." He replied. Billy nudged me and whispered, "he gets kinda scared about church sometimes." Billy was real good about taking up for his little brother. Peewee grinned then and said, "I'm scared the Holy Ghost might get me."

Billy just about fell over laughing then. "You know the Holy Ghost ain't gonna get you. You're scared you might get the Holy Ghost." Peewee just grinned again and they began rolling around and tussling on the ground. Peewee was such a good-natured little boy. He never seemed to get mad at anybody, or afraid either, so far as I could tell.

Then suddenly Billy jumped up and said, "I know what let's do! Let's just go around to the church and see if there's anything to be afraid of. C'mon, everybody who's not a scaredy-cat. We can just peep in and see."

The church Billy was talking about was The Church of God, which was on Clark Street, directly behind Twitchell Street. It was only about 5 minutes away if we cut through the neighbors' back yards. No one would even miss us. My better judgment was trying to warn me, but by now my curiosity was killing me. And besides, I couldn't let Billy know I was a scaredy-cat. Before I knew what was happening we were on our way.

Of course I had seen this little wooden church jillions of times before. I could even hear the people singing sometimes on Sunday nights when we were barbecuing in the back yard; but now as we crept up to the side door through the bushes it seemed so different. I knew it was not nice for us to snoop around when no one was there. My heart began to pound like it usually does about scary things but my curiosity took over again and by the time we had climbed the old wooden steps there was no turning back. I slowly pulled on the door handle, almost hoping it would be locked, but no, it creaked only slightly as I turned it and gave the door a gentle push.

I could tell Billy and Peewee were a little bit scared, too, even though they went to that church most Sundays and the preacher, Brother Coody, was sort of kin to them.

It was a little spooky just being in the dim insides of the church, imagining all sorts of spirits that might be watching us, but a more real fear for us was that Janie Carol Barrett, the neighborhood's most famous tattle-tale, might be watching from her house across the street and we knew what would happen if our parents found out where we had been. I think we all knew this was not really a good thing to do; we didn't know why, but we just knew our parents wouldn't like it, and were afraid we would be punished if they found out; but even that fear couldn't keep us away now.

As we began to explore inside, hardly daring to breathe, we were drawn, almost like by a magnet to the baptistery (I think that's what they call it) and without really stopping to think what we were doing, crawled right in and began pretending it was a swimming pool. Now that I think about it I believe that was a pretty sacrilegious thing to do, but it was prob'ly the most fun part of that whole adventure. I remember there was a scene of Jesus standing in a lake or river with people around him ready to be baptized I suppose, and this was painted so that the baptistery seemed to be a part of the scene and standing there it was almost like we were part of the scene, too; almost like being in a play.

It was kind of pretty but I was not real impressed. Even at that age I wasn't too crazy about the art work. Jesus' head was painted too big. Come to think about it, maybe that was just to make people understand how important Jesus is, but still I thought the painting just really didn't do him justice. Most of my school pictures are like that.

We decided we'd better not stay too long or

Aunt Howard would wonder where we were and we didn't want anybody to know what we had done this time. We were really lucky not to get caught. Maybe it was because I had been praying silently that we wouldn't and that God wouldn't be mad at us. I'm glad our Sunday School teacher had taught us how to pray silently.

It was pretty recently that I had my first important experience with prayer. Of course they taught us in Sunday School that prayer means talking to God and I had been saying the "Now I lay me down to sleep" prayer since I first began to talk but that prayer was not very helpful to me when I tried to go to sleep. In fact I always tried not to think about the part that goes "If I should die before I wake..." That would definitely not help me go to sleep. I prayed The Lord's Prayer in church of course, but I mostly just shied away from really religious stuff because I usually ended up feeling a little scared. I wondered, too, how you could love God when you couldn't even see him. Not that I would WANT to see him, of course. To me, God mostly seemed far away.

I had a lot of good experiences at Sunday School, but I didn't understand some of it. My favorite religious thing was for my mother to read Bible stories and poems to us kids, which she did almost every night. She could really make it all come alive; almost like being there. The only other time when God seemed real and very close to me was when I would go to a special secret place where there was a hole just the right size for me in the hedge between our yard and the Hands' yard, and when I sat there no one could see me and I would just think about God and wonder about things I didn't understand. I felt as if God was there with me and it was a good feeling that I've never forgotten. I even wondered sometimes if maybe God was trying to talk to me and I just didn't know how to hear him.

Momnee is a very religious person and she is a good person, too. One day not long ago when she came home from work she had a sad look on her face. I was old enough to realize that in her job as a field worker with the welfare department she saw a lot of situations that made her feel sad. She told us kids how the Depression was causing people to lose their jobs and sometimes their land and houses; she talked about going into homes where they didn't have any furniture, or even any food.

But that night was different. She broke down and cried as she told us about a mother who had two children, a boy and a girl, who were about our age. The little boy was in the Charity Hospital in Shreveport with pneumonia. He was very sick and the doctors thought he might die. I asked Momnee if there was anything we could do to help. I adored my mother and couldn't bear to see her cry and suddenly I began to feel what she was feeling for that mother and little boy. This was probably the first time in my life that I had strong feelings of sympathy for people I didn't even know. I even had tears in my eyes, too.

She said, "The only thing we can do for them now is pray and I hope you'll want to do that." That night I prayed with all my heart that the boy would get well; and the next night and the next... and on and on for at least two weeks. I had no doubt that my prayers would be answered. My mother came home from work one day and said, "Do you remember the sad story I told you a few weeks ago about a boy who had pneumonia? Well, it had a happy ending. He went home from the hospital today and he is going to be just fine."

I remember how glad I felt; happy, but not really surprised. I knew! I already knew what the outcome would be. I will always remember that feeling. I think it is called faith and I learned about it from real life. I didn't tell anyone I had been praying for the boy to get well but after that happened I had a different attitude about prayer and I don't think anything could ever shake my faith in it. Now God doesn't seem so far away. Some things you just have to learn from real life; like the power of prayer.

Now that I'm almost a teen-ager I wonder what it will be like when I'm grown up and fall in love and get married. Sometimes I think maybe no one will ever want to marry me. I might end up being an old maid like Aunt Howard. But maybe not; I can tell that some boys like me but the only thing that really worries me about growing up and being in love is that so often the people you fall in love with fall in love with somebody else. At least that's the way it is lots of times in books and movies; then things can get really complicated. I guess this is just one of those things that you have to learn about from experience. For instance, I wonder now if it's all right to pray for a certain person to love you; probably not, because he might not be the right one. I can see that being a teenager is prob'ly not going to be all that easy and being a grown-up is prob'ly even harder. Maybe I need to start praying for myself to understand more about God and to be a good person because I have learned some things already from real-life experience about the power of prayer.

Chapter 6

Childhood Christmases

Christmas Candles 1931

MY NAME IS Edith Joy Stothart, but everybody calls me E-Joy. I am almost fifteen months old, but of course I don't know that now. The only thing I know at this moment is that my daddy is holding me tight and I'm looking up, up at a big, tall tree with lights on it:

"See tree! See 'ights! E-Joy git 'ights." Daddy grabs my tiny arm just in time to prevent my busy baby fingers from grabbing the lighted candle I am straining to reach. I struggle with all my might to grab it. We are standing in the living room of my Aunt Mamie and Uncle Gray Stothart's house and I am gazing upward in amazement and delight at a vision that shuts out everything in the dark of that room except the glow on our faces and twinkling eyes; the glow reflected from flickering candles that light up an evergreen tree and the gleam of ornaments, both store-bought and home-made, hanging from its branches.

2016 Looking Back

I am 87 years old now, and many Christmases have come and gone since my very first Christmas impression from so many years ago. That tree must have been a glorious sight; a Christmas card come to life. They tell me it was a holly tree brought inside from the nearby woods. But the most potent memory-maker for me—in fact, the only thing I can really remember to this day—is the smell of melting wax from the twisted candles that lighted the tree. For me, always, the sense of smell is the most evocative of all the senses, calling up memories of the past. The candles on that tree, unlike the scented ones we buy today, were not infused with perfumes to give them the woodsy smell of pine, or the enticing aroma of spicy Christmas baking. Still, their natural waxy smell of paraffin and bees' wax remains with me today, more than eighty years later, bringing back vague dream-like thoughts and memories of long ago; a part of my own story of "Christmas Past."

I try today to picture a tree alive with the glow of real lighted candles, their soft beams illuminating everything within its radius, with its radiance bringing light where there was darkness; smiles to faces made weary by the drabness of everyday life and work. In a place where, too often, the distractions of this material world dull our senses to the wonder and beauty of the world of the Spirit, I imagine this light bringing all of us to the true light, the "Light of the World" that offers to draw us all, everywhere, into one great circle of love, at Christmas. May that light continue to grow until it brings us all into the love and joy and peace that was born with Him for all the world to share, at Christmas and forever.

Christmas 1934

I am thinking now of the Christmas when I was about six years old and Alexa was four. By that time our family had established a tradition that was a little unusual. Since Santa had such a long sleigh ride on Christmas Eve our parents put in a request for him to make his visit to our house early in the evening, which he agreed to do, on the condition that we children not be at home at the time. Santa's gifts were supposed to be a surprise, of course, so we children must agree to go to bed without a fuss when we were told to. Momnee and Daddy thought that would be a great idea and so did we.

While we were having supper Momnee read the Christmas story from the book of Luke, where the Angels sang to the shepherds, "Peace on earth, good will to men." Alexa's big brown eyes got bigger than ever, and she asked quietly, "What about the women and the little children?" Momnee explained that the angels' song was for *all* of us, today as well as way back then. I was glad of that and I'm sure Alexa was too. I always liked that story no matter how many times I heard it.

"Emily, why don't we take the children over to Gray and Mamie's to see their tree and visit a while?" Daddy said to Momnee right after supper. He put down the newspaper and reached for his coat and car keys.

"Why that would be nice, Bob; I'm sure they'd love that; wouldn't you? But we mustn't stay too long 'cause you know Santa will soon be here." She looked at us and we said, "yes! YES!" before they could change their minds. We delighted in going to Uncle Gray's and Aunt Mamie's house. He was Daddy's older brother and this aunt and uncle were almost like the grandparents we never had, to us. When we went to visit them they let us do lots of fun stuff.

"Maybe I should stay here to put out the wine and fruitcake for Santa and make sure the door is open," Momnee said, as she began gathering up coats and caps. "That's a good idea, Emily. We don't want Santa to miss this house, do we? Howard, if you'll come with us the three of you can sit in the rumble seat while I drive." Aunt Howard put on her coat. I think she was just about as excited as we were.

"Yay! Yay! It will be just like going for a sleigh ride, only without the snow!" We struggled into our coats and caps, climbed into the rumble seat at the back of the car with a little help, and were soon on our way, singing "Jingle Bells" at the top of our lungs. (All this for a two-mile ride across town.)

It was a cold night, but not *too* cold. Our coats and caps were warm and when the wind got a little chilly we just snuggled into the blanket Aunt Howard had thoughtfully brought along. We looked up at the stars and they seemed brighter than usual, and almost close enough to touch. "Do you think we can see the Star of Bethlehem if we look real hard?" I was talking to Alexa and she nodded, but Aunt Howard said, "That was a long time ago."

When we reached our destination Aunt Mamie and Uncle Gray seemed to be expecting us. "How about some hot chocolate and cookies? It's cold out there tonight," Aunt Mamie said, as she helped us with our coats and caps. We followed her back to the kitchen and she poured cups of steaming hot chocolate for us and served cookies. She made the best cookies. She made everything good.

We savored the rich, warm, chocolaty drinks and tea-cakes but our eyes soon fastened on the glittering Christmas tree. "It's so tall! ...So many lights!" Our voices rang out with excitement. Our tree at home was pretty but this one was taller. The gas light in the living room was turned down low and the colored lights on the tree glowed like magic beads in the darkened room. We listened to the radio a while and talked about what Santa was going to bring. Alexa and I danced to the music on the radio like we always did when we went to Aunt Mamie's and Uncle Gray's house and everyone clapped for us and before we knew it, Daddy and Aunt Howard were hustling us back into our coats and mittens for the ride home.

The house was dark when we walked in the front door and we tiptoed into the bedroom where Momnee was "sleeping." She still had on her robe and after she hugged us she said, "let's go in the living room and see if Santa has been here. I thought I heard something while you were gone but it might have been a mouse." We raced for the door, but Momnee got there first, and plugged in the Christmas tree lights.

"Oh, oh!" we gasped. As our eyes adjusted to the dim light we saw an amazing sight under the tree. There were two dolls dressed in velveteen dresses, one deep blue and the other cherry red, with white furry collars and muffs. When we got a little closer we screamed with delight. "Emilie and Annette! Two of the Dionne quints!" One for Alexa and one for me! We loved the Dionne quintuplets. Momnee had read to us out of magazines about the five little Canadian sisters whose birth caused such a stir around the world. When we played "pretend" I was always Annette and Alexa was Emilie.

There were other things under the tree as well; apples, oranges, hard candies, a peppermint stick for each of us, and a great huge slab of raisins in a big flat box. We saw only the dolls. Santa got it just right. We asked to take our dolls to bed with us and of course Momnee said, "Yes." The memory of the love that surrounded us that night will always be a big part of the Christmas Spirit for me. Good night. Merry Christmas. Peace and good will to all men, women and little children.

Looking Back, 2014

The Christmas season of 2014 proved to be "A Christmas to try not to remember" for Edgar and me. It all began in early December, with great promise, like so many of our more recent Christmases. A trip to Natchitoches to attend the Lessons and Carols service at the Basilica of the Immaculate Conception is one of the highlights of the season for us because we love the music of

Christmas, especially the religious music, and this year was no exception. The music was superb, but there was one tiny problem. The church was packed, and someone sitting directly behind us coughed constantly. We were determined not to let that ruin a great evening, but as it turned out, we spent most of the rest of the Christmas season in bed with flu.

It was not a fun Christmas, but it did give me time to reflect on past Christmases, especially those when I was a child. Our family knew how to celebrate Christmas. Even during those difficult years of the Depression and World War II the adults in our lives made sure we children were introduced to the traditions of this special season. I know without a doubt that after Aunt Howard came to live with us when I was about four years old she would have seen to it that no Christmas went uncelebrated. Aunt Howard never lost her child-like delight in holidays. She loved them all and Christmas was her favorite.

With the possible exception of the Christmas when we all had the flu, Momnee and Aunt Howard made sure that certain traditions of the Christmas Season were faithfully observed. There must be fruitcake: a fruitcake made immediately after Thanksgiving and doused once a week with wine or bourbon, with one slice reserved to be set out for "Old Santy Claus" (as Aunt Howard called him) on Christmas Eve accompanied by a glass of wine to strengthen him for the rest of his long sleigh ride.

There must be letters to "Old Santy Claus" as well. Aunt Howard brought out the big Sears Roebuck catalog to get us started thinking. We were warned, however, that our letters must not be greedy letters. Our parents reminded us that these were hard times and even Santa was feeling the pinch of the Depression. Greedy children would not be rewarded with a lot of toys. We soon learned that it was best to let Santa know what we really, really wanted most and then if we were lucky and very good we might even get something extra.

There must be a turkey: a turkey bought long enough ahead of the festive day to be fattened up in our own chicken yard and served up with southern corn bread dressing, gravy, cranberry sauce and other seasonal favorites on the big day. Although we were often lucky to get bread and milk for our evening meal during those Depression days, our Christmas dinner table was a bountiful one even during those hard times and Momnee arranged a beautiful centerpiece on the table with greenery and red berries from the yard or the woods and our best china, silverware, and crystal on the table (even if it didn't all match).

There must be stockings hung for the children, with or without a fireplace, and those stockings must have big fat apples and oranges and raisins inside with some nuts, a candy cane, and a few other candies, too; Santa and the Good Lord willing. It must have taken some sacrifices on the part of the adults of the household, but during the deepest dark Depression days and years the children of our household never felt deprived of the benevolence of "Old Santa." I'm sure there were many children in our part of the world who did. However, in small communities everywhere people seem to find ways to join together to help those in need in whatever ways they can. Hard times often bring out the best in people, and we seem to find ways to help one another.

There must be stories: Christmas stories told to eager children snuggled up in bed on cold December nights with quilts nestled all around. Stories about children who picked cotton to make money to buy Christmas presents for people they loved. Stories about children who picked up pecans to make Christmas goodies; about cedar trees dragged out of the woods and lighted with candles. Oh, how we loved those Christmas stories which Aunt Howard would begin telling us the night after Thanksgiving and continue with increasing anticipation throughout the season. Momnee read Christmas stories from the childrens' classics, like "The Birds' Christmas Carol," and "The Little Match Girl". One of our favorites was the long classic poem, "Twas the Night Before Christmas", which Neenie memorized from beginning to end, as a very small child, and recited for the family and then later

Illustration by Ellen Gaddis Howell

at the Methodist Church Christmas party. We listened to stories and begged for more.

After Momnee began working at the Welfare Office the "little house" grew larger and Momnee declared that we must have firelight so we sat around a crackling fire in our beautiful new living room fireplace on Christmas Eve eating Christmas treats and listening as she read The Christmas Story from the book of Luke in the Bible. We sang Christmas Carols and listened to special Christmas programs on the radio. We listened until we could hear reindeer hoof-beats and jingle bells on our roof and ran screaming and jumped into our beds so Santa wouldn't catch us up past bedtime on Christmas Eve.

On Christmas mornings dolls were always waiting under the tree for one, two, and later three little girls. Our living room suddenly became a gathering place for "celebrities" from everywhere. Shirley Temple rode all the way from Hollywood in that sleigh and surprised me one Christmas morning dressed in a fur-trimmed coat and muff. The next year Princesses Elizabeth and Margaret Rose made the sleigh ride from London to delight Alexa and me. Then came two of the Dionne quintuplets from Canada. They seemed to fit right in with our family, feeling completely at home under our tree and later in their window seat on the sleeping porch. When Neenie joined the family she started out with baby dolls and graduated later to ballerinas and a bride doll as I remember, and by the time Will came along he was begging for live dogs and a pony which, thanks to Daddy, he eventually got. I don't think the pony came by sleigh, though. Christmas was very merry in the "little house" on Twitchell Street.

Except for that one sad Christmas when we all had the flu and a visit from Dr. Davis and his big booming voice. That's the one Christmas I choose not to remember.

Aunt Howard's Christmas, 1936

The Christmas Season always started for Aunt Howard in early November, when the pecans had fallen off the trees. She loved making plans for Christmas. She would begin by telling us stories about when she was a little girl. If we promised to be good she would let us snuggle up in bed with her while she told about picking cotton to earn money for school clothes and picking up pecans to make Christmas money.

"What was Christmas like way back when you were a little girl? Did it snow then? Did Santa Claus come to bring you presents in his sleigh? What was it like?" We were full of questions and Aunt Howard loved to talk about Christmas.

"In some ways it was just about like it is now. I can't ever remember it snowing at Christmas time. Santa Claus came to see us, though, and we left fruitcake and wine for him just like you do. We had good things to eat and all our family got together for Christmas dinner. Mama played the piano and we sang Christmas songs; but in other ways it was different. We didn't often get toys for Christmas. Old Santa Claus usually brought things like oranges and apples and candy, and we sometimes got useful things like socks and handkerchiefs and underwear," she recollected.

"Underwear!" We both howled in disbelief. "I'm sure glad Santa Claus started thinking of better things to bring and quit bringing underwear," I said. "Did you and Daddy and Aunt Hazel and all the others act bad or something? Maybe that was why he did it."

"We were no better or worse than you kids today. That was just the way it was. But we didn't mind. It was still a surprise on Christmas morning and we probably enjoyed those things just as much as you do your toys. When children were bad back in those days they got nothing but switches and ashes in their stockings."

Alexa looked sad. "That must have been awful for them. I think Santa Claus has learned to be a lot nicer person than he used to be," she said. Aunt Howard chuckled, "Well, when I was a little girl, not as old as you are, that's what Christmas was like. It was a happy time. But then Mama died not long after my baby brother Claude did, it never was the same after that. We all worked hard and saved our money, and we always had some kind of Christmas but it was never like it was before Mama died." It was time for bed.

One cold November day Aunt Howard gathered up buckets and herded us out to the yard to bring in the pecan harvest. "We need to pick up all the pecans we can while the weather is good," she said, "because Christmas will be here before we know it. Let's see who can fill up their bucket first." After this word of encouragement the race was on.

We worked hard, hard, picking up pecans that day. My bucket was about half full. We worked so hard we had to take our sweaters off. We got tired, but Aunt Howard just

said, "Yes, siree, old Santy
Claus will be here before we
know it. We've got to get
these pecans picked up."

Aunt Howard stopped
for a minute and looked
at us. "Let me tell you the
main reason we need to pick
up these pecans. The main
reason is we need money
to buy Christmas presents.
After we crack and pick out
all the pecans we need for
our Christmas cooking, we
can sell what's left over to
get our Christmas money.

*The tradition of picking up pecans
with Aunt Howard continued into
the next generation. Aunt Howard,
Annie Ruth Jones, and Bob Gaddis
in 1954*

Now, what do you think about that?"

Well, that settled it for us. We didn't want to be left out
of Aunt Howard's Christmas plans. We got back to work
without any more complaints and by quitting time we
had picked up enough pecans to pick up Aunt Howard's
spirits considerably. We knew enough not to ask about
the plan yet; when she was ready she would tell us. In the
meantime it gave us something to wonder about.

December 1936 – Christmas Plans

It was mid-December. The days were getting cold after
a brief Indian summer. Aunt Howard had cracked
and picked out all the pecans we needed for the family

Christmas treats. The remaining ones had been sold and the money, our hard-earned Christmas money, put in a safe place. The fruitcakes had been baked and put on a shelf in Aunt Howard's closet where she tended them daily, splashing bourbon, bought for the purpose, over the cheesecloth-wrapped cakes as needed. The Christmas spirits were alive and well in Aunt Howard's closet.

Meantime, we had Christmas on our minds almost constantly now. At school the teachers started handing out coloring sheets with Santa Claus, reindeer, and Christmas trees on them. "Momnee! Look at my Christmas pictures I did at school today." I didn't even give her time to take off her coat before I ran to her and proudly thrust the day's coloring sheets into her hands. "My, what a beautiful Christmas tree!" she exclaimed. I liked to color the Christmas trees best because I could use many different bright colors on them. "You did a nice job on all these, but—look at this one! An angel! You drew this one yourself, didn't you? It's wonderful!" Aunt Howard was right, I thought. This will be the best Christmas of all.

We were having a Christmas play at school, soon. Alexa and I were talking about it when I came home from school one day. "Guess what! I'm gonna get to be an angel," I said. "You hafta be able to sing good to be an angel. I'm gonna sing 'Harp The Herald Angels Sing' with all the other angels. Our costumes are gonna be made out of sheets with tinsel wings and halos." "You're talking so fast I can't even hear you," Alexa interrupted. She talks a lot slower than I do, but she knows just as many words, and she wants to be sure you hear 'em all. She's smart, too, but she's not old enough to go to school yet.

I continued to gush on and on, not even listening to what she said. "All the boys want to be animals like camels and cows and sheep and a donkey. They like to make animal sounds but I don't think they're really s'posed to do that. Some of them have to be wise men and shepherds and they don't like that because they'll hafta sing, too." I like singing a lot. It's one of my favorite things. I like Christmas songs.

Downtown most of the stores had colored lights in the windows and toys and other things to buy for Christmas. You could tell Christmas was almost here. And then, finally – it happened: Aunt Howard got out the jar with the Christmas money in it, set it on the dining room table and divided the money among us. She said that wasn't quite enough, so she pulled her black purse out of its hiding place and added some more nickels to each pile.

"Now, it's time to make our lists. Joy, you're in school now, so you can write your own. I'll do mine and 'help' Baby Sister with hers."

I ran to get my red Big Chief tablet and three yellow pencils from my book satchel. "Now this is the way you do it," she said. "Write the names of all the people you want to give presents to. Then I'll tell you how much money you can spend for each one."

Christmas Shopping

It was December now and one Saturday morning the weather was clear and cold. The frost outside looked almost like snow. We dressed in our warmest clothes, including caps and mittens. We had our lists and money fastened carefully in our coat pockets as we skipped down the street to the Variety Store to buy Christmas presents. Aunt Howard was taking Alexa and me to do our Christmas shopping. There was ice on all the puddles and it was all we could do to resist testing to see if the ice was thick enough to hold us up. Aunt Howard was watching for things like that and soon laid down the law to us.

"Now, you'd better listen to me. Follow right behind me. Stay on the sidewalk. DON'T get in the street and DO hold my hand when it's time to cross the street. That's all. Unless I tell you something else. And no fussing and fighting or we'll turn around and go right back home. And when we get there I'll jump on both of you with all four feet." When we walked past Bee and Genie's store it just didn't seem right not to stop to buy candy, but we didn't say a word.

I'm glad she didn't just say, "Now y'all behave yourselves." It seemed to me that it was easier to be good when you knew what being good meant. And it also helped to have something exciting to do, like Christmas shopping. And besides, if we were bad Aunt Howard would not only make us go back home but she would tell Santa Claus. We knew she would. We were good all the way to The Variety Store. The store felt warm inside and there were already other people shopping. "Can I go to the aisle where the toys are?" I asked Aunt Howard. "Please. I know where to go and I won't go anywhere else. I promise." Alexa and I were both excited because this was a day we had been waiting for.

"I have a surprise for you," Aunt Howard said. She smiled and her eyes crinkled up at the corners. "Do you know what a balcony is?" she asked. "I think so," I replied, and I pointed up high toward the back of the store. And then I saw it! There was tinsel draped all over the wooden rail that went across the balcony. There were bright-colored Christmas decorations on it and on the Christmas tree that stood in one corner.

"That's where all the Christmas stuff is; all the things we're shopping for. Every year they put all the Christmas merchandise on the second floor, so that's where we need to go." She was right. There were lights on the stairs and a Christmas tree with colored lights on it. People were walking around up there. I had never noticed the stairs and the balcony before. It was like discovering fairyland. I couldn't wait to get up there and start my shopping. I got out my list.

I found a pretty handkerchief for Miss Huggins, my teacher, and a tiny bottle of toilet water for Momnee. I think it was called "Evening in Paris." There were lots of little china dogs and cats, and I knew Alexa liked that kind of stuff. I chose two little brown and white spotted china dogs for her. Maybe she wouldn't break them. She was always slow and careful about everything. She even talked slow. Yes, that would be just the right present for her.

I got a box of watercolors for the girl whose name I drew at school. I thought she would probably like them, but if she didn't maybe she would let me borrow them. That way my money wouldn't be wasted. I know I would like them because I like drawing and coloring, so I'd be sure to like water-coloring.

I pulled on Aunt Howard's sleeve. She was busy doing her own shopping and helping Alexa. "See what I got?" I interrupted, to show her my finds. "You're doing real good," she said. "Do you have many more presents to buy?" she asked. "Just two," I replied, hoping she wouldn't ask me who they were for; because one of them was her. It might hurt her feelings if she knew she was the last one on my list. So I asked her a question. "What do you think I can get for Daddy?" She thought a minute. "I think maybe a handkerchief or some shaving soap. He's gettin' kinda low on both."

I scampered off to find shaving soap. I had no idea where to look, but the ladies behind the counters were real nice about helping me. I soon found shaving soap, but what to do about Aunt Howard? I couldn't think of anything. I had just about given up and decided to get foot powder when I saw a funny looking contraption on the end of that same counter. "Excuse me ma'am," I said to the sales lady. "Can you tell me what that thing is?"

She laughed. "That is a pretty strange looking contraption isn't it? It's a back-scratcher," she said. "Oh, good! Thank you ma'am, I'll take it." I knew right away it would be the perfect present for Aunt Howard. She always needed somebody to scratch her back for her.

Now that we had finished our shopping Aunt Howard had another surprise for us. We walked all the way down Front Street to the Loreco Café, that Daddy owned, and ordered hamburgers. Aunt Howard had a Coke with hers, but Alexa and I had to drink milk. That was all right because the hamburgers were SO GOOD. We all loved hamburgers, especially Aunt Howard. She told them to put everything on hers, 'cause she loves onions.

I will never forget going Christmas shopping at The Variety Store with Aunt Howard. I'm glad we had sense enough to be good that day because the kids' Christmas shopping trip became one of our family traditions, until we got to be too grown up and sophisticated. Growing up has its price!

How Does it Feel to be Grown-Up?

I think it must happen when you are in about the sixth or seventh grade. Lots of things start to change then.

When I was in the sixth grade, and about eleven years old, I joined the Campfire Girls. We did lots of fun stuff, and we learned a lot and helped people, too. We had pretty uniforms that were red, white and blue, and we wore them to school on our meeting days. The first time I ever remember going Christmas caroling was with the Campfire Girls. I will never forget that experience. Camp Fire Girls opened up a whole new world for me!

Our first group leader (she was called our Guardian) was Mrs. Hattie Whittington, a nice lady who lived near the court house. Then we had another Guardian, Stella Susan Edgerton, who was still in college at the time. I admired her, loved her, and tried my best to be like her. (Never did succeed.)

We did lots of fun things while Susan was our Guardian; hiking and sunrise breakfasts that we cooked on an open fire; ceremonial fires in the woods, where we wore our ceremonial gowns and got honor beads for our achievements. Probably the thing I enjoyed most, though, was going Christmas caroling on one cold December night, just before Christmas. It was right after the Sunday evening church service, and we left the church by way of the steep outdoor stairs behind the choir loft.

As I walked out into the December night, the stars seemed almost close enough for me to reach out and touch them. I could see my breath it was so cold; good thing Momnee made me bring my mittens. I skipped down the steps with excited abandon, then paused as I heard singing; or thought I did; no, just my imagination. Maybe it was the stars singing to me, or the angels. That was such an amazing night; my first time ever to go caroling. Just to *think* of going caroling filled me with wonder and awe. I almost couldn't believe it was actually happening.

We tried singing as we walked, but it was not easy; the wind was blowing, and we began walking faster to keep warm. Sometimes it was hard for me to keep up; maybe because my legs were shorter than the older girls'. Susan, our leader, had made a list of people who wanted us to stop at their houses and sing to them. As we got nearer the homes where we were to stop we got very quiet so we could surprise them with our singing.

It was even better than I thought it would be; the people really liked our music. They said our singing was beautiful; sometimes they asked us to sing one of their favorite carols, and we knew them all. Most of the people we sang to were old, and some of them even brought out cookies for us to eat, or fudge. That night I found out that one of the best things about Christmas is the music; especially singing carols.

The last place we stopped to sing was the Boyds' house, which is right next to the Grade School. The Boyds are really nice people; they're real old, and they told us that they came to this country from England a long, long time ago. They already knew some of us because they go to the Methodist Church; it's right across the street from their house. Some of us go to their house after school and they serve us lemonade and cookies, only they call them biscuits because they are English and that's what the English people call cookies. When we go to visit they always remind us to phone our parents, so they'll know where we are.

Well, they were so surprised and glad to see us that night that they invited us to come in. When we finished singing for them they gave us mugs of hot cocoa and biscuits. (The English kind.) Then they taught us an old English custom; this is how it goes: You march around the dining table holding hands and singing the English carol, "Here We Come A-Wassailing" (Caroling.) The last verse of the carol goes like this:

God bless the master of this house,

likewise the mistress, too,

and all the little children that round the table go.

Love and joy come to you;

and to you your wassail too;

and God bless you and send you a happy new year.

Before we left we sang, "We Wish You a Merry Christmas," and Mr. and Mrs. Boyd told us that we had given them a beautiful Christmas gift. By that time we were pretty tired and pretty stuffed, so we went back to the church and our parents came to get us. I will never forget that night; ever since, I have always loved going caroling. Music is one of the most important things in my life and I think Christmas music is the best of all.

CHAPTER 7

Summertime

"Only the Rich Can Travel"

DURING THE Great Depression and throughout the troubled years of World War II few people except the wealthy and famous traveled regularly as people do today. Most people took trips only when necessary and only as far from home as required. Travel was expensive, a lot of trouble and often downright unpleasant. Ordinary folks had neither the money nor the leisure for it. You have to wonder why anyone even bothered. Why would you pack up a lunch, cram your family into a hot car and risk flat tires or other road breakdowns in that old flivver just to get away from home for a few days? Who would want to spend hard-earned money and meager vacation time just for a few unusual sights and fun experiences? Believe it or not some people did and our family was no exception. Why?

When the weather got stifling hot those little buzz fans didn't help at all. The radio kept blaring the bad news about breadlines in the big cities and of former tycoons jumping out the windows of skyscrapers. The war news from Europe got worse every day and the kids began complaining about having to help with chores in the house and in the "victory gardens." Finally something just seemed to snap in the minds of the parents. Maybe their better judgment deserted them temporarily and they thought things would feel better from somewhere else. Maybe they were right to think like that.

My daddy had a saying that I can remember him using all his life in all kinds of situations, and it always fit perfectly. He would smile with a kind of "knowing" look and say "only the rich can travel." It is amazing how many situations this saying covers. The first time I remember hearing Daddy say it was when Momnee convinced him to take us on a summer vacation to Hot Springs, Arkansas.

"Emily, I'll be back in about thirty minutes," Daddy says on his way to the back door. "Try to have the kids and the suitcases all ready to go. I'm on my way to pick up the lunch box and I'm gonna get Shorty to look at that right rear tire again. It looks low to me." Daddy's whistling now as he hurries out the back door and that means he's in a good humor. We're all in a good humor because we're getting ready to go on our vacation trip to Hot Springs. That's way up in Arkansas and this is the first real vacation our family's ever been on. Sometimes at Christmas we go down to Jennings to see our kinfolks in South Louisiana but this is different. We're not going to visit anybody; we're just going to have fun! Momnee says we're going to see lotsa interesting stuff and we're takin' our bathing suits so I know it's gonna be fun.

We're all in the car now. I shouldn't say "all" because we're leaving the two little ones at home with Aunt Howard. I'm sure glad Alexa and me are big enough to go. It's fun riding in the car; Daddy has the windows rolled down and it feels good with the wind blowing my hair all over the place. Momnee says it's gonna be a long ride, and I can tell it is because I'm already getting kinda tired. But it's gonna be fun.

"I'm going to suggest that you girls might want to get out the paper dolls you brought with you now because it really is going to be quite a long ride. Later on it'll be fun to look out at the scenery but right now you're going to have to entertain yourselves and not bother Daddy because he has to pay attention to the driving and keep us all safe," Momnee says. I learned a long, long time ago that when Momnee suggests something you really are s'posed to do it so we get out those paper dolls and play for a long, long time, until we're getting kinda tired of that. Finally I start seeing a lot of buildings so I ask if we're almost there.

"Oh, no, not yet," Momnee says. "We're just now getting to Shreveport. See, over on the right. That's Barksdale Field; you should remember it from when you've been up here shopping with me, or to the doctor's office. It's going to be quite a long ride but we'll take a little bathroom break in a minute and then I'm going to suggest that you try to take a little nap, or play the 'I Spy' game," she says. I think I see now what she means about it being a long ride.

"What's happenin', Momnee?" I ask. All of a sudden she's shaking me awake from my nap in the car and we're still on this long trip to Hot Springs. Only now we're stopped at a place that looks kinda like a gas station and I can hear Daddy's voice but he's not in the car. He's outside talking to a man and it looks like they're taking the tire off our car. Oh, no, I'm thinking. We must have a flat tire. Daddy and that man look real hot and sweaty.

"C'mon, honey. You and Alexa had better get out of this hot car with me and we'll find a shady place to sit down. I'll see if I can buy us something cold to drink." Momnee is waking both of us up.

She's talking to Lexa now, and we're both awful hot and sweaty. Momnee is explaining to us that we're in Texarkana, Arkansas, and have a flat tire on our car that's got to be fixed so we can drive it the rest of the way to Hot Springs. Yep, I knew that was prob'ly what was happening and Daddy sure doesn't look happy. He's saying some cuss words now but things are not real bad yet because we're out of the hot car and Momnee's sitting down with us now under a big tree where it's nice and shady.

When we finally get back in the car we still have a long way to go but it's beginning to get exciting now because when we look out of the car window everything's beginning to look more and more different. We can see lots of hills and they're getting higher and higher, and I think maybe they might be mountains, so I ask Momnee if we're gonna get to see mountains with snow on top but she says "no," and she's usually right. She says these are hills but they're lots higher than the hills we're used to seeing where we live and one of them is even called Hot Springs Mountain.

I think we went to sleep again for a while, but now

that our long trip is over we've found a place to stay in a "Guest House" in Hot Springs. It just looks like a big ole house to me but the sign says "Guest House" and it doesn't cost all that much to stay here and it's close enough for us to walk to where all the Bath Houses and shops and things are. There's lots of huge hotels and some Tourist Courts that look like tiny little houses that are all connected together. It costs a lot to stay at those places and it really doesn't matter to us where we stay because about all we're gonna do at this house is sleep and eat breakfast. We'll be out seeing things and doing things. That's what Momnee says.

It's morning now and Momnee is making sure we get to see all the important sights so we're gonna get to go inside the Arlington Hotel, and the Majestic Hotel and at least one of the big Bath Houses on Bath House Row. I can't understand why people would travel a long way just to come and take baths. I ask Momnee about it and she says it's because the water comes from special mineral springs and it makes people get well from their rheumatism and stuff like that. They can get massages for their muscles, too, but I'm glad we don't have to do that kind of stuff. This afternoon we're gonna go downtown and do some shopping and then tomorrow will be prob'ly the best part of this trip. We'll get to spend the day at Fountain Lake!

Lexa and I get to have hamburgers for lunch but Daddy says, "No siree, Emily, I cook and serve hamburgers every day at the cafe so you and I are going to splurge a little and have a steak. Only the rich can travel." Momnee laughs and he does too. Soon as we finish eating we start our shopping but Daddy says, "Take your time, girls and look around; see everything you can see, because I'm afraid your money's not gonna last very long."

At first we mostly just walk around and look in the windows of the shops and souvenir places. They have all kinds of interesting things to buy in the shops (Daddy calls 'em "tourist traps") and most of the stuff has "Hot Springs, Arkansas" written all over 'em. We just have a little bit of money to spend and we've been dying to go in and see all the stuff up close. Momnee says we might find something to take home to Aunt Howard and the others since they couldn't come with us. Maybe we'll each get a souvenir to remind us of the trip, too. When we go in the shops we see there's lots of stuff to buy but according to Momnee most of it is pretty tacky. I think she's right and it doesn't even seem very useful either. Finally we find a candy shop where they let you watch from a window and see the people making the candy. It looks good and smells real good too. We get some for Aunt Howard because we know she'll like that and it's fun to watch the people making it right before our very eyes. We can give away some of the beautiful crystals we picked up when we went walking up on the mountain. We have way more than we need.

Looking Back, Fountain Lake

Probably the part I enjoyed most about the whole trip to Hot Springs that summer was Fountain Lake. That was most likely because of the special interactions with my parents that experience involved. Alexa and I spent much of the time in the swimming area with Momnee, who began teaching us how to swim. I could remember her swimming with us a few other times but there were always so many other people around that I didn't think of it as a special mother/daughter time. This time she gave her whole attention to us and just helping the two of us learn to swim. At first it was a little scary but then as I relaxed more and more it got to be fun. I actually began swimming a little that day.

Then in the evening we spent our time on the dance floor in a pavilion built out over the lake. There was music, of course, and that helped to make it special. At home on Saturday nights I loved listening to the Hit Parade on the radio and often made up my own dance steps in our living room, with Momnee and Daddy watching. But this was the real thing.

Now those same Hit Parade tunes were coming out of a Juke box right here in this pavilion, with the moon and stars shimmering on that mirror of lake that we could almost reach out and touch and my little sister and I were watching our parents dancing to the music. We could tell they were having fun because of the looks on their faces; it was almost too good to be true. Then my daddy actually asked me to dance with him and began showing me how to do the real dance steps that fit the music. Learning to dance was much easier than learning to swim; probably because it didn't involve putting my head under water.

I never would have thought my daddy would ask me to dance on a real dance floor with him. I was glad Daddy was such a good dancer because that made it easy for me to follow him gracefully around the dance floor. It was so easy and fun that I felt as if I had been dancing all my life. I took dancing lessons when I was five years old but I will always remember that it was my daddy who gave me my first real ballroom dancing lesson on that dance floor at Fountain Lake.

That was a very exciting vacation, my first real trip, and an adventure with lots of happy things to remember. I don't remember anything about the trip home, however, except that Alexa and I were careful not to say unkind things to each other and Momnee suggested that we take naps so we slept a long, long time.

Momnee, Neenie, Joy, and Alexa on later trip to Hot Springs

Magnolia Park, Magical Summer

During the years of the Depression and World War II, vacation trips were luxuries that were out of reach for most families. The lucky ones had their own alternatives, such as grandparents living nearby or a cabin or camp house on a lake or seashore just a quick drive away. For our family's answer to survival during the blistering heat of August in a small house crowded with children who were tired of playing in the back yard with nothing for relief but a splash in the garden hose, there was a place called Magnolia Park. Oh, the joy of it! We could get there easily in a couple of hours, it was affordable, and it was our oasis in the summertime desert called Coushatta.

This is doubtless true of many of the pleasures in life, but I believe it is especially true of trips: the anticipation is almost half the fun and it begins to seem more and more real as we make our plans and we see and hear and take part in the preparations going on all around us. This is certainly true of us children in the Stothart household as we prepare for our summer excursions to Magnolia Park. The smell of chicken frying in the kitchen for our picnic lunches and a cake baking in the oven to take along; the hustle and bustle of getting out our suitcases and putting in our coolest pajamas and playsuits; the excitement of the last couple of days are almost too much for us to bear. Or maybe it's just me; it was certainly true for me as a child. The edge wore off the excitement as I grew older and learned to enjoy the anticipation as just one of the stages of travel fun.

When we went to Magnolia Park it was sort of like an expedition. Families often went in groups, which increased the fun. Neighbors got together and planned it that way. That way, we could always socialize with people we didn't already know if we wanted to but it was nice to know there would be people there that we knew, enjoyed being with and were comfortable with. Yes, a lot of it was about comfort. Comfortable clothes, (except for those itchy wool bathing suits and of course we had to endure those because that was all we had) food that was easy to fix and maybe not even healthy; picnic food. We even took paper dishes. No housekeeping; I'm not sure there was even a broom in our cabins, and I am sure we didn't take one with us. We took big old beach balls and maybe a few board games just in case it rained but I don't remember that ever happening. The mothers mostly took a lot of magazines, decks of cards and novels, and those who smoked brought their cigarettes, of course. We could all just relax and enjoy being there, every minute of it; that was what Magnolia Park was for.

Getting to Magnolia Park was not a big problem because it was not far away; that two-hour ride seemed much longer of course because we just couldn't wait to get there. The time that we actually spent being there seemed shorter than it was because we were having so much fun. The minute we turned off the highway we began looking for familiar sights and markers along the dusty gravel road. There were not many of those because Magnolia Park was essentially a nice, shady spot with a big pond—we preferred to think of it as a small lake—in the middle of a Central Louisiana pine forest. But we didn't want to miss the little road that turns off before you come to the sign up over the road that says, "MAGNOLIA PARK" in big letters.

We know we're here now; we don't even have to ask because there's the sign hanging over the roadway and our car is drivin' right under it. I'm beginnin' to see some of the cabins now and I wonder which one will be ours this time.

"Oh, look, y'all! I can see the waterfall now, and the water wheel. I wonder if any of the kids sittin' there under the waterfall are anybody we know from last year. I can't wait to get out and get my suit on and get in that c-o-o-o-l water." I can no longer contain my excitement.

"That water's not cool, it's real cold," Alexa says. I didn't even think she was listenin' to me. Sometimes she doesn't. When the car finally comes to a stop at "our" cabin we don't even offer to help get all the stuff out; we just grab those wool bathing suits and head for the house to pull them on. The next thing we know is we're gaspin' for breath as we plunge into that cold water. I do see some kids I recognize from last year but I don't remember their names, or where they're from. That's okay. We'll find out tomorrow.

1980's Looking Back, Magnolia Park: Where Did it Go?

Edgar and I are driving south on US highway 71 several years ago, on our way to some kind of event—I can't remember exactly what—and I notice a sign on the left, just an arrow pointing left that says: MAGNOLIA

PARK. I'm about to doze off, but that gets my attention and I yell "Slow down, Edgar. Please slow down." As he follows my instructions with an anxious look on his face, wondering what kind of emergency I'm experiencing, I try to explain to him what that place means to me as I plead with him to please, please slow down and help me try to find it. By this time we have pulled off the highway and are slowly making our way down this little gravel road in the piney woods and I can tell by the slightly disgusted look on his face that he is trying to find a suitable place to turn around.

"Please," I implore. "I haven't seen that place in almost half a century, but I know it's out in these woods somewhere. I never expected to see it again in this lifetime. Those were some of the happiest times of my childhood." I'm using my most pitiable but persuasive voice. (Crying would be taking it a level too far, because we're headed to an "Event" in Alexandria and I don't want to mess up my eye make-up.)

My whining finally works, but we are not able to find Magnolia Park this time. Maybe later; or maybe it's just as well we can't find it. This way it will probably remain forever a mystical chimera; a wonderful Shangri-La memory of my child-mind that could never measure up to the real world expectations of an adult. When I think of Magnolia Park and tell my grandchildren about it I will tell them what the experience was for me at the time: a cool shady Eden in the middle of a pine forest with rustic cabins sprinkled among the trees; a waterfall with a water-wheel and a place to swim; a pavilion where teens danced to a juke box; and a bonfire on a rare cool August night complete with ghost stories being told with sound effects under the trees to young, unsupervised children in smelly, wet, moth-eaten wool bathing suits. I will tell them about children of all ages running around without much adult supervision and going to bed tired but happy. And children on the way back home to Coushatta making plans for next year.

2015 Looking Back (again)

Today Edgar and I are having lunch in one of our favorite hang-outs for the elderly, the Red River Council on Aging "Depot Diner," which is housed in the old Railroad Depot in the middle of downtown Coushatta. We love to eat lunch here, because, not only is the food good, but we're also likely to see good friends and neighbors at this place who will gladly share a table with us, and if we're really lucky, we might also happen to see someone whom we haven't seen or heard from in years, who is visiting friends or relatives in Coushatta. It happens sometimes.

Sitting at the table next to ours today is a couple almost a generation younger than us, whom we know well, Diane and Alvie Slatton, eating and talking with a Representative from the State Legislature who lives in the Alexandria area, and with whom we are also acquainted. They are speaking with some animation, their talk punctuated frequently by bursts of laughter. There is no way I can avoid overhearing the name, "Magnolia Park" come up repeatedly in their conversation. I am, of course, fascinated. It is inevitable that we join that table and conversation and to my delight I discover that not only are they all three familiar with my old personal childhood "Disneyland" but they are even happy to verify my description of the place and match my tales with some of their own, to the amazement of my incredulous husband, who has long ago decided that the place exists only in my childhood imagination. What a great ending to that mystery of long ago.

Childhood Candy Land

Even though the people who lived in our neighborhood didn't get to go on summer vacation trips much, we children found interesting things to do closer to home, during those summer days so free from the busyness of school activities. Sometimes on summer mornings the kids in our neighborhood would get together on the wide front steps of Fred Jr.'s house and dump our pennies and nickels out to see if we had enough money for a trip around the corner and up the street to "Bee and Genie Bernstein's" neighborhood store to buy candy. Making our plans was almost as much fun as the trip itself.

"How much do you have Marcia?" asked Fred Jr.. "Ante up. We hafta be sure everybody has some money or we can't go. I'll put my nickel in the middle; that's the way you're s'posed to get the pot started." (I know what he means because sometimes I listen to my daddy and his friends when they play poker in our dining room.) He pulls a nickel out of his pocket and plops it down on the top step. Fred Jr. always has the most money because he gets an allowance. Marcia tells me to go ahead and put my money on the step. She's untying her pretty white handkerchief with the rosebuds and lace on it. I put my two cents beside Fred Jr.'s nickel. Alexa puts hers next to mine. Billy and Pewee each lay down two pennies.

Marcia pulls two nickels out of her handkerchief. "Gol-lee, that's good, Marcia, you have a nickel more than me!" Marcia plunks her two nickels down next to Fred Jr.'s. Then she pulls three cents back from the pot. "Aw! What'd you do that for?" Fred Jr. looks disgusted, but Marcia doesn't let that bother her. She looks Fred Jr. right in the eye and says, "Fred Jr., Daddy gave me that extra nickel yesterday when he came by to see us. I'm saving two cents for the church collection and one for Sunday school." She stares straight at Fred Jr. with a calm look on her face and smiles the prettiest little smile. He just says, "Oh." I really do admire Marcia. She's so pretty and she can handle Fred Jr., too.

Now we start thinking about what we want to buy today. It's kinda hard because there's so many choices: Tootsie Rolls, Kit Kats, B-B Bats, suckers on sticks, rolls of Lifesavers with a lot of different fruit flavors. All of us have our favorites. Most of these candies are five or ten for a penny. By putting together two cents each, plus Marcia and Fred Jr.'s nickels, if we plan carefully enough we can buy enough candy to last us for at least an hour (if we eat slow).

Bee and Genie Bernstein are an old, old Jewish brother and sister—one of only two Jewish families in town—who live in the back of this little general store they opened up in our neighborhood years and years ago; probably even before I was born. If you need something on Sunday like a loaf of bread you can go to Bee and Genie's to get it because they're the only store that's open on Sunday. Maybe that's because they're Jewish. It must have been Jesus who started Sunday, but maybe not, because my Sunday school teacher said Jesus was a Jew and she's usually right about things like that. Bee and Genie are not completely Jewish because they put wreaths in their windows at Christmastime and Jews don't usually do Christmas things; at least not the same way Methodists and Baptists do.

No matter how many times we've made that trip to Bee and Genie's it's always an adventure. We like going there but there's not a one of us who would go by ourselves. The store building itself is a little spooky; an old brown house that looks a little bit like I imagine the ginger-bread house in the story of Hansel and Gretel looked. It has a front porch with a swing that one or the other of the owners is usually sitting in when we got there. If it's "Miss Bee" who sticks out her bony fingers to greet us it REALLY makes me think about the story of Hansel and Gretel. She could be the witch with her brown wrinkled skin that looks as if it might crackle and flake off if you touch it. Her long black hair is streaked with gray and pulled to the back of her neck in a bun with strands falling out all over the place. She's sort of bent over and little and bony, but her eyes and her smile are nice and she's real nice to us so we don't feel afraid of her. She always seems glad to see us; maybe we're her best customers; maybe her only customers?

Illustration by Ellen Gaddis Howell

2005 Looking Back

I am an old lady now, but I remember one of our trips to buy penny candy as vividly as if it happened yesterday. It started out like all the rest of our candy-buying trips but ended up with sort of a different twist. When we got inside the store the sights and smells in that place made our mouths water and we were glad we had money to spend. The sharp smell of sausages and cheese, the yummy chocolaty and fruity smells of the candies and their bright-colored packages pulled us like a magnet— straight into that store.

On the counter, big round glass jars with hinged lids on the front seemed to jump out at us with their bright colored treats inside, just waiting there for us. There were suckers that looked like little round pieces of bright colored glass stuck onto sticks. I could always smell the cherry kind real good. One jar had big round spicy cookies with hard white icing; they were good but you could only get two for a penny. We passed them by as we looked for a better bargain. The Depression taught people, even kids like us, to be what Momnee called "thrifty shoppers."

Miss Bee was patient with slowpokes. Some of us had a terrible time making a decision and handing over those scarce, hard-to-find pennies. I know because I was one of the slowpokes. When we finally pointed out the ones we wanted she reached a trembling hand into the jar and filled a small bag for each of us.

By the time we had all been helped, a shuffling sound got our attention and we all turned and looked toward the velvet curtain with little beaded strings on it that served as the doorway to the rooms where the Bernsteins lived. Mr. Genie was pushing his way through the beaded curtain to say "hello." He looked even older than Miss Bee and tremblier too. His smile was hard to tell from a frown because his long nose seemed to almost touch his chin. We always tried to look behind that curtain to see what was on the other side but that was a mystery we never unlocked.

As we waved "goodbye" to our friends, the storeowners, we hopped, jumped and chased one another down the steps. We raced down the sidewalk, being careful to jump over the cracks. We rounded the corner across from

Florane's Filling Station, where we saw "Miss Emma" Florane sweeping the concrete in front of the store she and her husband own. She speaks French almost as good as English and they used to have a ferry boat on the river that took people and cars across the river which is just a short piece down the street from their service station. After the bridge got built they didn't use the ferry boat any more.

Sometimes we walk down to the bridge and look at the river when we go to buy candy but we didn't have time that day, so we ran down another street, past the big chinaberry tree and the cow lot until finally we plopped down panting and sweating onto the steps of the Scheen house again and began to divide up our treats.

One reason our candy lasted so long was that we always picked out kinds that came in five-or-ten for a penny packages; but the main reason was the way we divided it up. It was kind of like a game. We spread out the packages, opened them up, and each of us had a turn to choose one piece until they were finally all gone. After that, we still could swap with one another if it was okay with both people. It was not a bad plan, but it just took so LONG.

We had just got started on the swapping part when a door inside the house banged and Mrs. Georgia Scheen, Fred Jr.'s mother, who was a long, lanky lady, took several big giant steps across the front porch just in time to see us poking our candies and candy papers back into the bags as fast as we could. But we were too late. Lifesavers rolled everywhere. We had guilty looks on our faces. We were caught red-handed. No way to escape.

"Fred Jr., where in the world have y'all been? I've been looking everywhere. Well, of course! You've been to the Bernstein's store again without asking. Dinnertime is just an hour away, and here you are about to stuff yourselves full of candy. Well, no siree; not this time. Maybe you'd better just give the candy to me." She sounded really cross now.

"Aw, Mother, PLEASE. You can't take it away from us now. That's not fair. We spent our own money for this candy. I promise we'll save it until after dinner. Please, please!" None of the rest of us would help Fred Jr. with his pleading. We were all just a little bit scared of his mother; she had a temper and she wasn't even a redhead like me. But she was a nice, pretty lady and she almost always gave Fred Jr. whatever he asked for because he was an only child.

"Well, if you promise. But I don't want you ruining your dinner. Beulah has fried a chicken, cooked fresh peas and cornbread and made a berry cobbler for dessert." Fred Jr.'s mother disappeared into the house almost as quickly as she had appeared like magic just a few minutes ago. She probably had to go in and supervise Beulah the cook as she finished getting dinner ready. It was almost time for Big Fred to get home for the noon meal.

"Boy, that was close," Fred Jr. said as he handed us our bags and stuffed as much candy into his mouth as possible. Our trip to the candy store was more of an adventure than usual that day. Maybe we should think of a better place to divide up our candy next time; maybe we should tell somebody where we're going; maybe we will next time if we don't forget.

Summer Reading

I was pretty young when I discovered that summers could be a lot of fun for a child who had the freedom to explore and experience the world without an excess of adult supervision. Summers presented me with a lot of free time. The perception that children were safe in our own homes and backyards remained prevalent in our little town during the 1930's despite the continuing publicity surrounding the kidnapping of the Lindberg child in 1932 and the trial and execution of the killer. After all, that was a unique and isolated case, involving a family who were wealthy and world-famous. It could never happen to us. Thank goodness it never did.

Thank goodness for the freedom. We felt safe; we didn't live in a world of fear; in a little country town we played alone or in the company of our neighborhood pals. No adults yelling at us and telling us what not to do all the time; but as I look back now I know that they were there—just invisible to us. They were watching; so many of them. They would have intervened, any one of them if they had seen or sensed any danger signals. We never complained about "nothin' to do" because if we did those adults became all too visible:

Momnee on Saturdays, planting flowers:

" . . . There're lots of weeds to pull";

Aunt Howard, hanging out the wash:

" . . . Hand me those clothes pins, now;"

Mary in the kitchen:

" . . . I need you to dry these plates for me, baby."

And Others:

"etc., etc."

My typical summer passed all too quickly without slipping into the doldrums of boredom and discontent. I soon learned that the easiest way to prevent that problem was summer reading. That's when Nancy Drew came to my rescue. I think adults today call it "Beach Reading." I might not be able to travel to distant and exotic lands and find new friends to join me in exciting and perilous adventures, but I could join Nancy Drew and her friends in her never-never land where anything could happen and often did. And if some adult tried to pry me away from the challenges that faced Nancy Drew and me, I would be too far away to even hear their cry. I would be under a shady tree, following Nancy wherever she went, and not entertaining a thought about boredom.

I must have been nine or ten years old at the time and reading well enough to enjoy chapter books. I had encountered The Bobbsey Twins series earlier at the Coushatta Grade School library. They were probably the first series books I ever read and I liked them because when I really enjoyed a book it always irritated me to come to the end and lose my relationship with the characters who had suddenly become my best friends. Then I was relieved to find them again in the next book of the series. When I read my first Nancy Drew mystery and discovered it was part of a series I thought I had died and gone to heaven. I am almost certain it was my best friend, Robbie Sue Adams, who introduced me to Nancy. This was a blessing for all three of us.

I don't know how or where Robbie got her first Nancy Drew book; I think it was *The Secret of the Old Clock*, but as soon as she finished it she passed it on to me and from that moment we both became enthusiastic fans and collectors. To this day I enjoy reading not only series books but mysteries as well. I prefer the "soft" mysteries, but have also read and learned to enjoy other darker, more sinister mysteries if they are not too gory and hair-raising for a wimp like me.

There was no public library in Coushatta to satisfy this appetite for Nancy Drew Mysteries that had grown to be almost an addiction for Robbie and me, but my mother, who worked for the Welfare Department had to go to Shreveport to regional meetings fairly often and she became an "enabler" for our habit. She would make a trip to the bookstore after her meetings and look for the new books in the series as they came out and they came out often.

CHAPTER 8

World War II

Strangers in Town

"GUESS WHAT, Lexa! Daddy's gonna invite his friend, Major Monholland to come to our house for Sunday dinner. Isn't that exciting? He wants him to come and meet Momnee and us kids, and eat with us, too. I've never met a real army major before and you haven't either. I think he's stayin' over at the hotel now – you know – our cousin Erkie's hotel, but Daddy's gonna help him find a place to stay for a longer time so he can bring his wife and two little girls here. They need to live here in Coushatta for a while because the army's gonna have something here called maneuvers, but I don't understand about all that. I just heard Daddy and Momnee talkin' about it after you were already asleep last night." (I don't think my little sister is listening to a word I'm sayin.)

"Well, I don't know Daddy's friend you're talkin' about, so I guess you'll have to explain it to me. If you want to." Alexa is prob'ly too young to understand a lot of the stuff I tell her, but I think she'll be just as excited as I am when she finds out more about those two little girls who are gonna move here.

"I think maybe Daddy'll have to tell you all about the Monholland family, Lexa but I can tell you that Daddy said the girls would prob'ly be good friends for us to play with because they're about our age. And they have a dog, too. I can't remember the girls' names, but you'll never believe what the dog's name is. It's Geoffrey McTavish Monholland; it's a Scottish name because he's a scotty dog and the girls wouldn't go off and leave him for anything in the world because they love him so much. They'll need to find a place to live where they can keep their dog with them. I sure hope Daddy can help them." I'm saying all this to Alexa, but she still doesn't seem too interested. What she says is, "I just wish he'd let us have a real puppy instead of those ole bird dogs of his." I do, too. The bird dogs are nice, and kinda fun, but they don't seem like real pets.

2005 Looking Back – Clouds of WWII

A few months after Momnee's death in 1999 my two sisters and I spent several Saturday mornings going through her books, papers and filing cabinets in order to decide who should get what and what should be thrown away. During this process we found a letter written by a Major Monholland and sent to our dad from somewhere overseas during World War II. It immediately caught my attention and brought back pleasant memories of playing with his two little girls during their brief stay in Coushatta.

It also brought back other wartime memories from my childhood; some frightening, some pleasant and others interesting and bittersweet.

I remember one day when Alexa and I were eating our lunch at the Loreco Café. Daddy and Major Monholland were eating together and talking about the Louisiana Maneuvers, which were scheduled to begin soon in our area. I was listening to their conversation and I heard him laugh and warn my daddy not to run afoul of Captain George Patton, adding that it would definitely be a mistake to make him angry. I got so interested in their conversation that I forgot about the time and I guess Daddy did too, because a few minutes later he jumped up, and said, "Oh, dang, it's five after one. I'm gonna be late getting my girls back to school. I hope they won't be in trouble."

On hearing this Major Monholland stood up and motioned to his orderly who was sitting nearby. "Put these two little girls in my jeep and drive them to the Elementary School and escort them to the office with my apologies," he said. That short ride was one of the most exciting events in my young life. I hoped all the kids sitting in all the front classrooms in that building were watching as we were accompanied up the long front walk and right up the steps to the entrance of the Coushatta Grade School by that handsome young man in uniform. I was thinking: "I can't wait to write about this in my diary." And we didn't even get in trouble for being late.

I found out years later that the Captain whom Major Monholland was talking about became "THE General

George Patton" who was head of the 2nd Armored Division, known as the "blood and guts division" that played such an important role in the World War II campaigns in North Africa. About fifty years later my husband, Edgar, told me an interesting tale about his mother doing laundry for Patton and some of his men during the Louisiana Maneuvers in the summer of 1941. Edgar was just a child at the time but he remembered that these soldiers rewarded his family with food as they cleaned out their camp when they left the area.

The Monhollands soon found a home in our little town for their family and the dog with Mrs. Shirley Stephens, an elderly widow, and her sister, who lived in a large home across the street from the Methodist Church. Alexa and I did become friends with the little Monholland girls. I remember the older girl who was my age. Her name was Josephine but she was called Jojie. I don't remember the younger one because Jojie and I probably ignored her and Alexa, but most of all I remember Geoffrey McTavish Monholland, who was a very proper Scottish dog and didn't even bark much.

Not long after that, after Britain became more deeply involved in the war, I met another new friend because of the War. She attended school at the Coushatta Grade School because her parents, like so many others, sent their child to this country to escape the horrors of the London Blitz. I didn't get to know this little girl well because she was not in my classroom but I played with her at recess and identified with her because she had reddish hair and freckles like me. I thought a lot about what it must be like to live in a city where bombs were falling every night; where you had to leave your home and go to air-raid shelters, sometimes in the middle of the night. What would it be like to be sent half-way across the world to live with strangers so that you could be safe from the bombs?

This child was living in the home of a wealthy family in Coushatta and was well cared for and treated with great kindness but I thought how frightening it would be to wonder if your parents and friends back home were safe. We heard news of the bombings being broadcast over here every day on the radio, and saw scenes that appeared on news reels at the movie theater constantly. As I played with this little English girl under the big oak trees on the playground at Coushatta Grade School, I thought of how much she must miss her loved ones and worry about their safety. I wondered if war could happen here to my family. Getting to know this little girl, made the war even more real to me than hearing President Roosevelt talk about it on the radio in his "fireside chats;" even more real than seeing those news-reels after the main movie feature at the "Hollywood Theater" in Coushatta.

Louisiana Maneuvers

In late 1941, Fred Scheen, Jr., the unofficial leader of our Twitchell Street bunch began screamin' in our unimpressed ears: "The games have begun!"

"I'm tellin' y'all. I—been tryin' to tell y'all, but you won't listen to me. It's war games, is what it is. That's how they teach soldiers how to fight in a real war. I asked my daddy and he told me all about it. Well, maybe not all, but everything he knew. I'm not just makin' this stuff up."

Today Fred Jr. is so excited that he's almost yellin' in our ears now, so I guess it really is true. It has a name. It's called "the maneuvers" but "war games" really does describe it better. That's kinda what my daddy said. We can hear the roaring sound of those great big army tanks going by on the highway and when you get closer to 'em it sorta makes the ground shake. Big Fred, who is Fred Jr.'s daddy, told him that the soldiers are putting up little tents they call "pup tents" on the sand bar over across the river for them to sleep in. He said it looks like an army camp over there. I sure would like to go and see that, but I wouldn't dare go without asking Aunt Howard, and if we ask, I know she'll say, "no."

"Hey, y'all, I've got an idea," I say. "Why don't we just play like we're soldiers havin' maneuvers this morning; Fred Jr. can be the general of the red army and Billy can be the general of the blue." I think this is the best idea I've ever had for us to play, but before I even get it out of my mouth good, Fred Jr. jumps in with his own way of thinking about it.

"Well, instead of playin' like we're playing war games, why not just play like we're having a real war, like when we used to play cowboys and Indians?" he says. Well, I've gotta admit that does make more sense, but for some reason I just don't feel good about playing like it's a real war. Besides, how would we decide who'd have to be the Germans? I sure wouldn't want to be a Nazi.

As it turned out Aunt Howard was just as curious about the unusual activities going on down on the sand bar and under the Red River Bridge as we kids were. After she finished her chores and had some free moments when she would normally have been taking an afternoon nap, she agreed to chaperone a group of wide-eyed youngsters who were looking for their first glimpse of life in the military. We couldn't believe how lucky we were.

None of us could have ever imagined the sight that greeted us as we completed our short walk. It was like nothing we had ever seen before. What we found was a whole new world awaiting us on the banks of the familiar Red River. To our innocent eyes it could have been the whole U.S. Army camped down by the riverside. It was a sea of tents, uniformed men, jeeps, and military equipment. Fred Jr. had stumbled upon his earthly heaven.

Thank goodness, that day Aunt Howard had the good sense not to worry about us getting lost in the crowd. We didn't worry either. This was perhaps the biggest thing that had ever happened to the Twitchell Street Bunch. For some reason I don't understand as I look back, we were given the freedom to roam around among the troops, to talk to them, and to ask them questions. As for the poor bored young soldiers, they were obviously unoccupied with any specific duties right at this moment and seemed happy to have anything to entertain them. Even a bunch of rag-tag neighborhood kids.

Fortunately for us, we had brought my little sister "Neenie," along. She was barely more than a toddler clinging onto big sister's hands and singing all the popular songs of the day. She knew them all by heart and needed very little encouragement to perform for such an appreciative crowd. It was almost like having "The Hit Parade" right there on the sand bar. The applause alone would have been enough but these well-behaved young soldiers began pulling out all kinds of souvenirs and handing them out. Some of them even sang along with her. No one in the Twitchell Street bunch would ever forget that day. One of the men was introduced to us as "Donald Duck", and he talked to us in the exact same voice that we had heard on so many Saturday afternoons in the Walt Disney comedies at the Hollywood Theater in Coushatta. We were enchanted.

We were not the only gawkers to visit that military campground on that day and for several weeks to come. The men were welcoming to us townspeople; we were just as welcoming to them. As the war clouds hung over us we were beginning to develop a real sense of "we're all in this together" that was almost palpable. Sometimes they gave us candy bars and samples of their rations that they ate when they were having sham battles. As a child in the midst of all this preparation for war and talk of its proximity, I felt an excitement mixed with awe as I viewed this crowd of uniformed men, tinged with a vague sense of comfort in knowing that here were a lot of nice young men, some of whom I had met and talked to personally, whose job was to protect us and our country and to know also that they were learning how to do that right here in our town, and right now.

"THIS IS REAL, y'all! I'm Tellin' Ya Now, It's Real!"

The bright blue sky overhead made a brilliant background for flashes of sunlight that glinted off the shiny metal wings of a small airplane that maneuvered itself in darts and turns that reminded me of a small bird trying to escape from a hawk. The children of Twitchell Street watched in amazement, craning our necks to see what was going on high above our heads near the banks of the Red River.

"You see, I told y'all they were having a sham battle! You didn't believe me did you? See, there's another plane almost on top of that one. How can they come that close without hitting each other? They're having a dogfight just like we saw in the picture show. Gosh! This is the most exciting thing that's ever happened around here, I guess." Fred Jr. was all out of breath from excitement and showing us how smart he was.

"What is a sham battle?" I asked, knowing that I would be laughed at for showing my ignorance. But I really did want to know. "They're not going to drop bombs or anything like that are they?" I asked.

"Well, what do *you* think, dummy? Do you think I'd be standing here in the middle of the street if they were going to drop real bombs? I'd be running for cover. And anyhow those planes aren't bombers, they're fighters. They shoot at other planes. It's called 'dog fights.' I guess girls just don't know much about war. A sham battle is a pretend battle like when we used to play cowboys, remember? And sometimes they really do drop pretend bombs, too, but it's just sacks of flour so they can tell what they hit." Fred Jr. seemed pretty sure of what he was talking about. I believed him but I still didn't understand what it was all about.

We stood gazing up at the sky enjoying the spectacle like some kind of game, when suddenly, before we knew what was happening the two small planes collided and burst into an explosion of searing yellow-orange flames. Black smoke was gushing from the tail of one of the planes and the next thing we saw was both planes plummeting to the ground like wounded birds crashing onto the riverbank in a blaze of fire and smoke.

All of us gasped and looked at each other in amazement and fright. It all happened so fast. We didn't know whether to run home and hide under the bed or just try to find a grownup who could tell us why such things were happening, right here where we live. Was it a sham battle like Fred Jr. said or was it real? It looked real. And if it was real did that mean that the Germans had come to take over our country like with those other countries in the newsreels?

At that moment Aunt Howard came running gasping and breathless down the street, balancing my little brother, Will, on her hip. She had taken him for a walk down to Bee and Genie's store, where she joined a group of people gathered near the A. Hazard Perry Bridge that crossed the Red River. They were watching a convoy of army trucks crossing the bridge and setting up camp on the sandbar across the river. From there they had seen the same terrible sight that we had seen, only from a little closer view.

There was something I wanted to ask but I was afraid to. I was afraid I already knew the answer. "Was that a sham battle like Fred Jr. said?" I finally asked Aunt Howard, "or was it a real plane crash? What happened to the men who were in those planes?" Aunt Howard waited for a few minutes before she answered. She was still panting and gasping for breath, but I could tell she didn't want to talk about what had just happened; I didn't want to either, but I had to know. I prodded further: "This isn't a real war with the Germans, is it? They're not going to invade us are they?"

Then I thought about the day the teachers at school made everybody line up and march out to the big front porch with the tall columns and sit on the concrete steps to listen to people on the radio talking about the war in Europe. It was when Hitler and all the German soldiers marched into Poland and started killing the people. The British and French rulers declared war on the Germans and we got to hear about it on the radio but I couldn't really understand it all. I didn't think our country was in the war, but I wasn't sure.

Well, finally Aunt Howard got calmed down and figured out what to say, but it didn't make me feel very good: "This is not a real war," she said. "It's kind of a practice for war. But what you saw happen was real. Those were real airplanes and they really did crash. There were real pilots in them and they probably got killed in the crash. Yes, that's what happens in a war."

I shivered. I felt sort of hot and cold at the same time. My hands were sweaty and I felt a little bit sick. I had never seen anybody get killed before. I didn't know what I was supposed to say or do. I felt like crying but I didn't want people to think I was a cry-baby.

"I'm sorry the men got killed," I said. "I sure hope we won't have a real war in our country. What would happen if we had a war and our side didn't win?" I asked.

Aunt Howard took my baby brother Will's hand and started walking toward the house. "I hope we never have to find out the answer to that question," she said, and the way she said it scared me.

The next day some of the kids at school brought pieces of burned parachute and parts of the burned planes that they had picked up on the river bank near where the planes crashed. I was glad Momnee didn't let us go and see it. The smell of the burned parachute made me feel sick; I probably won't ever be able to forget that smell and the sight of those planes on fire. I don't see why anyone wants to have a war. I hope nobody I know ever has to fight in a war. But I think they probably will.

December 7, 1941

The glare of the sun almost blinds me as we step out of the dark movie theater into the afternoon sunshine of a blue-sky-beautiful December day. I head across the street toward my daddy's "Loreco Café" guided by my friend, Ruth Lester, who's handling the glare much better than I am. Finally I come out of my semi-trance when Ruth jerks on my arm and pulls me in the opposite direction toward the drugstore.

Ruth Lester and Joy

"Did you forget?" she asks. "Aren't we gonna walk down to the drugstore for an ice cream cone? I'm so hungry my insides are beginning to stick together after sittin' in that picture show for two hours. C'mon, let's go."

"I'll have to go across to the café first to get some money from Daddy." (I know it's rude to be so pouty but I just wish I could get an allowance like Ruth, but I always have to ask Daddy for money instead.) Ruth is a whole year younger than me, but her parents trust her to manage her own money. I'm goin' to talk to Momnee about it again. It embarrasses me to think that my parents are treating me like a baby; I'm even more embarrassed for my friend Ruth to know.

It's when we turn to walk back in the other direction that I realize something is wrong. A whole bunch of cars are parked around the service station and people are standing out in front of the café, talking. They're talking way too loud and seem kind of excited.

"Hey, look," Ruth says as she points toward the crowd. "Your daddy must be givin' away free hamburgers this afternoon. There's more cars over there at the café than at the picture show. Let's find out what's going on."

I'm sort of holding my breath, because I have a feelin' something terrible has happened; maybe somebody died, or somebody's house burned down. I always hate hearing bad news. I haven't seen this much excitement around here in a long time. 'Specially on a Sunday afternoon.

It doesn't take long for us to find out. Everybody's talkin' about it. As we get a little closer I hear the word, "Japs", and then something about "Pearl Harbor." Inside the café the radio is blaring, and people are sittin' at the counter and some just standin' still as statues, listening. When anybody starts to say something everyone says, "shh!" and they all get quiet; back to listening again. It sounds like President Roosevelt who is talking. Finally Daddy realizes we're standing there and he comes over to talk to us.

"Why don't you girls go down to the drugstore and get you some ice cream cones? Then I'll get Shorty to take you home," he says, pulling some money out of his pocket. Shorty is the real short colored man with the shiny-black smiling face who works for Daddy at the Service Station. He's always smilin', even when Daddy yells at him, and sometimes it looks like his smile covers his whole face. You'd like him; everybody does, even Daddy, although it seems like to me he bosses Shorty around way too much.

"But Daddy, what's happening?" I ask. "What're they talking about on the radio? Where is Pearl Harbor? When we came out of the picture show we saw all the cars and wanted to find out what's going on." (We've almost forgotten about our ice cream cones now.)

Daddy looks at us in a serious kind of way. "Oh, well, you're gonna find out soon enough; I might as well go ahead and tell you now. The damn Japs have bombed our ships in Pearl Harbor. It's in Hawaii. We're in the war now for sure. I don't have time to explain it all to you now; got to get these people served. Get your Mama to talk to you about it when you get home." Daddy has a look on his face that I recognize right away. It means he's upset, and that means it's time for us to go somewhere else.

I knew it was bound to be somethin' terrible; I knew it as soon as I saw all those cars and the people standin' around. I think you call it a premonition. Aunt Howard would just say she could feel it in her bones. I guess there's not anything more terrible than being in a war. Even the double-dip ice cream cones don't help my feelings about something like this. I don't like scary things. I'm prob'ly a coward. I hate to admit it but I am. I don't like the word, "war." When I see things about war on the newsreels I just want to hide my eyes.

When we get home, Momnee comes to the front door to give us the bad news. She tells us the Japanese have bombed our Naval Station at Pearl Harbor and some of our ships got sunk and some of our sailors have been killed. I try to remember if I know any sailors. I can't think of any. I know Mr. Roy's son, Maxie, who's in the Marines and my cousin Rex in the Coast Guard, but I can't think of any real Navy sailors that we know. There are different kinds of sailors, you know.

I'm glad Mr. Roy's son isn't in the Navy because I've had a terrible crush on him ever since I got my first haircut at his barbershop when I was five years old. His picture was hangin' up there on the wall right next to the mirror with his cowboy suit and hat and boots on and he looked just like one of the cowboys in the movies. I still think he looks like a movie star only I guess he has on a Marine uniform now. I know he's way too old for me anyway because I'm just barely eleven, but still I wonder where he is. He's my cousin Rex's best friend. And besides, I like Mr. Roy. He's nice; 'specially since I don't have to go to the barbershop anymore. I get permanents now instead.

Momnee has the radio on so we all sit down with her to listen. I have a million questions but I'll save them for later. I'm thinking now about the day we saw the two planes crash together and how I wondered at the time if that was real. That's one question I don't have to ask this time. I know, this time it is real. I can tell what's happening is important and even the grown-ups are all upset.

I don't know how I feel about it; kinda sickish; kinda scared. I feel like I want to cry, but nobody else is crying and anyhow I guess I'm too old for that; it wouldn't be appropriate. Will everything be different now? Will things ever be the same again? Maybe they'll tell us all about it at school tomorrow and then I'll understand. But will that make me feel any better? Or will it make me feel worse? I'm thinking about the English girl who went to our school for a while last year because of the London Blitz. I wonder if the Japanese will soon be bombing our cities. Today is Sunday, December 7, 1941, and I don't think I'll ever forget this date. I think some dates just stay in your mind forever.

2001 Looking Back at Pearl Harbor

No, I never did forget, and neither did anyone else who was old enough to understand what had happened that day. My cousin, Rex Stothart, came home from Newfoundland to his wife Louise, after the war. But his best friend, Maxie Smith didn't make it back. He died in the thick of the fierce fighting on Iwo Jima. Rex and Louise named their first child, Carl Max Stothart, for him.

Many years later on another quieter Sunday afternoon in our back yard, my husband's older brother, Herman, would tell us the sobering story of what it was like to be a sailor on a ship in Pearl Harbor on December 7, 1941; to be one of the "lucky ones," who came through that terrifying experience of violence unscarred – on the outside at least. His ship, the USS Dale, was the first to get out of the harbor after the attack.

Much later, on the morning of September 11, 2001, I am in bed recovering from open-heart surgery. Edgar phones me with the news that a plane has just crashed into one of the twin towers of the American Trade Center in New York City. I turn on the TV and watch in horror as another plane crashes into the second tower and as both towers eventually collapse. And I "remember Pearl Harbor." I know that millions of others are also remembering.

A Wartime Christmas – 1944

"Christmas got here so fast this year," I say to Alexa as we drop our schoolbooks on the table in the big front hall. We head to the kitchen for a snack, hoping there's something good in the pantry or fridge, because we're both tired and starved. It's Friday afternoon and the school Christmas holidays have just begun.

"Whatta you mean by that? It's not Christmas yet," she replies, "and it seems like to me it'll never get here; you must mean because the holidays have started, huh? Well, it won't really seem like Christmas to me 'til Aunt Howard starts makin' the Christmas cookies and stuff. Besides, my brain's still all crammed with stuff I memorized for two tests I had today."

She grabs a stool and climbs up to get crackers and peanut butter, and then something pops into her mind and she almost falls off the stool. "Oh, gosh! We should be hearing from Martin and Gene pretty soon about their Christmas visit. I sure hope they can get that leave and come here for Christmas. I can hardly think of anything else ever since we wrote and invited them. I wonder if anybody has been to the post office today."

I'm just sittin' here thinking how much I love this big old high-ceilinged kitchen, and how nice it is to have a house now that's big enough that we can invite guests over for holidays. After we moved here from the little house on Twitchell Street Momnee modernized the kitchen a little but she kept the beaded board ceiling and it's still a big, old-fashioned house; the kind of house I love. It's fun to invite our friends here because there's lots of room to do all kinds of stuff. It was so crowded at the little house that we hardly had room for the family, much less room to invite friends. Now sometimes after ball games, or movies, Alexa and I ask our dates and other friends to come home with us and make waffles, or sandwiches. Momnee and Daddy are usually okay with that as long as we don't get too rowdy. I'm thinking it will be great to have our soldier boyfriends here at Christmas time.

"Oh, I know what you mean about Christmas taking a long time to come," I say to Alexa, coming out of my daydream world. "They even have a saying about that, remember? We sometimes say a person is 'slow as Christmas.' don't we?" As soon as I say those words I wish I hadn't because I tend to forget how sensitive my sister is about her southern drawl; she just can't stand it when

The Big House

people tease her about it. She certainly doesn't have a pretend southern accent, like some people do; she just naturally talks slow.

"Now that Christmas vacation is here, I am getting impatient to see those guys again." (Actually I'm beginning to get a little impatient with Alexa, too; sometimes we're just not on the same page at all. Being impatient with her is sort of getting to be a habit with me. I guess if I'm honest with myself I'll have to admit that I'm envious of her because she's so pretty; naw, that couldn't be it.)

"Alexa, we don't have much time to get ready for Christmas and I want our house to look prettier for Christmas this year than it ever has, with Gene and Martin coming. And the Christmas tree...well, I kinda wish we could buy our tree this year so it would look like the ones in the magazines. Wouldn't that be great?"

"Well, no, I don't think so! Not really," Alexa says. "You know we can always find a pretty cedar tree in the woods and it doesn't cost anything. And besides, it's more fun to get our Christmas tree and it's always pretty. And besides, that's a lot more fun than buying one off of a parking lot at a grocery store, and prettier, too."

"No, it's not! Sometimes the ones we get are kind of scraggly," I snap. She's probably right, I guess, but I like to do new things sometimes. I guess I'm feeling a little more grown up since we've moved into a bigger house. It just makes life more exciting...although I...

Alexa just ignores me and goes on, saying, "I think it's more fun to go to the woods for the tree and who cares if it looks like the ones in the magazines? I just wish we could still get Hershey kisses to eat on our Christmas tree expedition like we used to before the war. Remember how we used to eat a whole bag of Kisses on the trip, and the whole family would come along; well, all the ones who were old enough, and we'd sing Christmas songs; well, all the ones who were old enough. Anyway, we don't even know for sure that Martin and Gene will get to come. They may not have gotten our letters yet. And what if they can't get passes or leave for Christmas? I don't think we'd better get our hopes up too much."

"Yeah, you're probably right." I have to agree with Alexa, even though I can hardly bear the thought that they might not get to come. "Well, I know they'll come if they possibly can. Who would want to be in a gloomy old army barracks at Christmas, with their homes and families so far away." I'm determined that "our soldiers," the ones we met last summer and spent so many happy hours with at the ball games and dancing at the Rec Center, will be able to spend Christmas with our family this year. It will be so exciting, and patriotic, too! "They've just got to come, Lexa, or I'll be really disappointed." I look at her now for reassurance.

"I want them to come just as much as you do," Alexa says, "but I feel just a little bit uncomfortable about it, too, in a way," she admitted. "I'm not sure what kind of things they'll want to do. We've never done anything quite this grown-up before, and it makes me feel a little bit anxious. I know we'll be going to all the usual church stuff. Well, what I'm thinking is, Martin is Catholic, you know. I'm sure everything will be okay, but I'm just a little nervous about it. We don't even have a Catholic Church in Coushatta. I'm not all that worried about the tree, or how the house looks. I just want everybody to feel good about everything and to have fun. Why not just be our-selves and do things the way we always do? I think they like us just the way we are." Suddenly I realize that my little sister is right, but of course I can't say that. Instead, I just say, "Oh, heck. Let's just get started planning."

"Yeah, and just not worry about any of that other stuff," she agrees. So that's what we're doing. I'm glad Alexa's going to try not to worry. She's always been a natural-born, first-class worrier. Christmas is no time to be worrying about things; especially when you have important guests coming. Guests from the U.S. Armed Forces.

"Hi! You two look like you're talking serious business. Can I get in on it, or is it top-secret?" Momnee surprises us by sticking her head in the kitchen door. She's a little late getting home today. I wonder if she heard any of our conversation.

"We're just talkin' about Christmas plans," Alexa explains. "We want it to be really special this year, because of Martin and Gene coming. And we really want them to feel at home here since they can't be with their own families at Christmas."

"Well, sure you do, and so do I. Can I help with the plans? I feel really sorry for those GI boyfriends of yours, being so far from home at Christmas. They're not much older than you kids, and expecting to go overseas anytime now. They're bound to be a little bit homesick at this holi-day time. I'm glad they're coming to spend Christmas with us. Just let me take off my coat and get a cup of coffee and we'll try to think how we can make it special for them."

Momnee's a good listener; I guess you could say a good sport, too. We can talk to her about almost anything.

She might say "no" to a request, but she doesn't make you feel like a dummy or a criminal for asking. It's almost like talking to one of our friends.

"Well, what are some ideas you've thought of?" Momnee asks. "I'd like to hear what you think about it first. I don't really even know these young men, so you might need to fill me in a little bit first."

We each look at the other like . . . "Go ahead and say something!" Can we talk about making changes without hurting Momnee's feelings? Sometimes adults can be sorta "set in their ways." Finally, Alexa decides to speak up:

"We just sort of wonder if we could maybe skip some of the church stuff this year, since Martin is Catholic and, you know, might not be used to the way we do things at our church." It gets quiet, and all of a sudden I'm wondering what we could skip. I've never really thought about skipping any of the family traditions. Church has always been a big part of Christmas for our family. What would it feel like to cut out some of the church activities? It makes me feel strange now just thinking about it. My first thought was it might be kind of grown up and sophisticated, but now it just seems a little sad; almost scary. I really like most of our traditions; especially singing the Christmas carols. I love all the Christmas music.

Now Momnee is looking up at us, and if her feelings are hurt she sure doesn't show it. She just says "Well, that's something to think about. You girls are old enough now to have some input into how we celebrate Christmas. Maybe it's time for us to think about giving up some of the old traditions, or add some new ones. We don't have to do everything the same old way forever. Some families even go out to a restaurant for Christmas Dinner. Joy, what would you like for us to change?"

Well, now I don't know what to say. This isn't going quite right; not exactly the way I had in mind. Suddenly I feel almost like crying. I can't believe she said that about going to a restaurant. I wish we could just forget this whole discussion. It makes me remember a long time ago, when Momnee tried to add a new tradition to our Christmas dinner. It went like this: As I remember, the table looked just beautiful with the good china, a Christmas centerpiece of evergreens and red candles. We asked the Christmas blessing and then Momnee served cream of mushroom soup for a first course before she brought in the turkey and dressing. Well, did that ever go over like a lead balloon! We made faces and Daddy just pushed it aside, so Momnee quietly removed it from the table. I felt so sad that her feelings were hurt on Christmas Day, but that was one time I was on Daddy's side. Needless to say, cream of mushroom soup never made it to our "Hit Parade" of family traditions.

Now Momnee is sitting here waiting for me to answer her question. I can't think what to say. Finally I blurt out, "Maybe this is not a good time to change anything. Why don't we just do it pretty much like we always did in the past. We've always had great Christmases, except for the year we all had the flu." (There! I feel much better.)

"Before we make any hard-and-fast decisions why don't we think about a couple of things: first, let's think about your friends. They'll be our guests, so we want them to feel welcome and at home with us. Can you put yourselves in their places? If you were going to visit their families at Christmas, what would you want them to do? How would you want things to be?" Momnee waits for an answer. (Silence.)

"Would you expect them to try to celebrate Christmas just the way our family does?" Momnee continues. "No, of course not." We both answer at the same time. "It wouldn't be fair to ask them to change their Christmas traditions. Things like that are too important," Alexa says.

"Yeah, and besides, maybe it'll be fun for them to see how our family celebrates. I guess we could just give them a choice about whether they want to go to the church stuff or not. I guess the main thing is just to make them feel at home and as comfortable as possible." (I'm feeling much better now.) But I can see that Alexa still isn't quite sure. "What if they decide they don't want to go with us to church? What do we do then?" she asks.

"Why don't we just cross that bridge when we get to it?" Momnee suggests. "Besides, something tells me it won't be as much of a problem as you seem to think. If they choose to visit our family at a special time like Christmas, I bet they'll want to go where we go, and do the things we do. I think they'll just be happy to be with you girls, and grateful to be with a family at Christmastime."

I can tell Alexa's feeling much more relaxed about our plans now that Momnee has gotten involved. Now I become the worrier. The thing I begin to worry about is, will Aunt Hazel be coming? Aunt Hazel really doesn't have any family except us, and she does like to be with us at Christmas. We like for her to come, too, and she really brings us nice gifts, but the only thing is, sometimes when she gets here, you can tell she has had way too much to drink; that makes Daddy mad, and when Daddy ... well, let's just say, we don't want that to happen.

It's not that Daddy objects so much to people drinking, it's just that Aunt Hazel is alcoholic and you really never know what to expect when she starts drinking, or where it will all end up. For that matter, you never quite know what to expect when Daddy gets mad, especially when he gets mad at Aunt Hazel or Aunt Howard. For some reason he seems to get madder at them than at anybody. I think it must go back to their childhood. Maybe they tried to boss him around. Or maybe he just remembers how bad it was for all of them after their mother died and their big sister, Aunt Maude, who was really just a child herself, had to try to take care of a house full of kids. Maybe their daddy had a drinking problem; who knows? I sure don't, but I just can't help wondering. Maybe I'll study psychology when I go to college someday so I can figure out stuff like that.

"You look like your mind is a thousand miles away, Joy. Do you have plans for tonight, or can we talk some more about our Christmas plans?" asks Momnee. "Christmas plans! Christmas plans! Everything else can wait." I can feel myself getting into the Christmas spirit again and somehow I have the feeling that everything's going to be okay; even better than okay; probably wonderful. We're all laughing now. Yes, everything's okay.

"Well, now that all that's settled we'll just relax and enjoy the Christmas Season," Momnee says, "and maybe it will help if we remember to think of the needs and feelings of others, first, whoever they are, but especially when they're our guests.

After supper as Alexa and I are getting ready for bed, she says, "I'm glad Momnee is so understanding about our problems, aren't you? Some parents seem to think stuff like this is a waste of time, or a bother. I have friends who never talk to their parents about important things."

"Yeah, and isn't it great that she has decided we're old enough to make our own decisions on important matters like Christmas? Some parents always make you do it their way."

"Yeah, I guess we're pretty lucky to have a mother like Momnee, aren't we? And just think about it: when she was our age she didn't even have a mother, or a daddy, either. It's a good thing she had grandparents; I think they must have been good grandparents." I'm glad my sister and I agree about some things.

It's hard to plan for Christmas festivities during these war years. Gasoline and tires are rationed and cars are old and run down. Of course Aunt Howard has been saving food ration stamps for some time. Christmas is important to her. You just can't make the holiday favorites like divinity, fruitcake, cookies and pies without sugar and shortening. This family hasn't had anything sweet since Thanksgiving, and that was kind of slim this year. We didn't mind; we had Christmas to look forward to, but many of the store-bought favorites like Hershey bars, chocolate Santas, peppermint canes and Gold Bricks are almost things of the past. While cigarette smokers suffer because "Lucky Strike has gone to war," kids miss their treats. But nobody complains. That would definitely be unpatriotic. And we think of the men who are sacrificing everything to keep us safe.

"Alexa, do you think we might get Daddy to stash away some Hershey's Kisses at the store for us to take on our Christmas Tree Safari?" I ask one day. By now we have heard from our boys in uniform and they are definitely coming for Christmas. "Maybe just this once he'll give in and sacrifice his ethical principles to make us happy."

"No, definitely not and it would be crazy to ask, unless you enjoy hearing him rant and rave," she replies without skipping a beat. "You know how Daddy is about stuff like that; like it's unethical for his family to have stuff his customers can't get; like it's black-marketeering, or something. He might do some things the church frowns on, like playing poker and drinking a beer now and then, but when it comes to business he has his principles. You've heard him say it a million times."

"Well, it wouldn't hurt to ask," I argue, knowing all along that Alexa is right. Come to think of it, she often is. It's almost like she was born knowing some things that a lot of us never quite get. I wonder if she'll always be like that. I think she prob'ly will.

"Just let me know if you decide to ask him so I can make sure I'm not anywhere in the vicinity," she says, and I decide maybe I won't push something so relatively insignificant. After all, there might be more important issues we'll need his consent about. And even though Alexa never says "I told you so" I sometimes wonder if that's the meaning of "that look" she gives me.

I was so right, or maybe just lucky. The very next day I realize that I'll need to borrow the family car to pick up the boys at the bus station. It's either that or get one of the parents to do it. They could walk I suppose; they've done it many times before, but that wouldn't be right since they'll be our guests. Driving to the bus station is at the very top of my list of important things to do.

I'm only fifteen, but I'm a legal driver. I'm so glad you can get a driver's license in Louisiana at this age. Momnee taught me to drive because when Daddy tried, things got unpleasant for both of us. So far I've acted pretty responsibly about using the car. By that I mean I almost never ask to drive. I only drive the car when it's absolutely necessary. Believe it or not, Daddy actually said "yes" this time. Maybe it's because he remembers when he was so far from home in France during World War I and he feels sorry for these poor guys and wants them to feel welcome, or maybe it's just easier this way; who knows?

Today as we drive to the bus station it's chilly and raining. "Good thing we didn't let them walk from the bus station. If we hadn't planned so well Daddy would have probably offered to pick them up, and wouldn't that have been awful?" I almost shudder to think of it. We're craning our necks every few minutes to see if the bus is crossing the railroad tracks even though it's not due for another ten minutes. Well, sometimes buses do arrive early. We sit and wait in the car in front of Bill Wilson's Drug Store/Bus Station for what seems like hours, talking about our plans for the day.

"We'll probably need to postpone the trip to get the Christmas tree. There's no way we can go this afternoon in this rain. Oh, well, maybe tomorrow . . ." We both see the bus pull up at the same time. It is exactly twenty minutes late. In the anticipation of welcoming our heroes we don't even notice that the rain has stopped and the sun is peeping out. The excitement in the air now is electric.

"Look, there they are! They're here! They're actually here!" We don't dare jump out of the car and run to meet them. Hugs and kisses are definitely out of the question on Main Street in Coushatta. In the early afternoon right in front of the Drug Store . . . ? Not even the banner of patriotism is broad enough to cover such a scandalous display as that; too bad, though; it would be fun to see the shocked looks on people's faces. Even if Alexa and I were silly enough to display such behavior our young service-men have better sense than to risk offending parents and townspeople so flagrantly. They know they're lucky just to be able to spend Christmas in the home of hospitable friends, and they aren't about to push their luck.

How silly of us to worry about how to make this a won-derful Christmas celebration, for us and for our guests. Christmas is here at last; our plans are coming together. We can see our handsome young military "heroes" stepping out of the Trailways Bus—and it feels wonderful.

Looking Back – December 25, 2000 It's
Christmas again!

I will never forget the joys of those Christmas Holidays of 1944. The boys enjoyed everything as much as Alexa and I did, although none of it was all that special. Just the things we normally do at the Christmas season. We went to church with the family and our guests went along with us. We found the most beautiful Christmas tree ever, and decorated it together. We all sat around the fire together and read the Christmas story from the Book of Luke, and sang carols.

One day while Gene and I did some shopping, Martin and Alexa spent the morning picking up pecans in the back yard. We had a huge pecan tree that was no telling how old, and the trunk of that tree was at least three feet in diameter. It was a native pecan and produced little tiny nuts, much smaller and tastier than the ones in the stores. Aunt Howard wouldn't use any other kind in her Christmas delicacies. She would sit for hours cracking and shelling them. Alexa and Martin spent the afternoon packaging a box of those shelled pecans to send to Martin's mother in Oregon. They don't have pecans in the Northwest. Of course the package didn't arrive in time for Christmas, but his mother was delighted when she did get them and wrote a beautiful letter thanking Alexa for the gifts and for inviting Martin to visit in our home.

Our Christmas dinner was a huge success. The platter of golden brown turkey and cornbread dressing made a magnificent spectacle as Aunt Howard brought it proudly to the table. The light in our eyes rivaled the light of the candles as we turned off all the electrical lighting and sat down to a bountiful feast whose aromas had been tantalizing our senses for hours. Being from Portland, Oregon, Martin had never eaten cornbread dressing before. He ate it as if this might be the only opportunity in his lifetime to enjoy this delicacy. Gene, on the other hand, said cornbread dressing made him a little homesick for his family in Marietta, Georgia. That didn't seem to spoil his appetite for it, however.

After dinner we opened gifts, but the gifts were never the most important part of Christmas to our family. I think that was partly a result of growing up in the Depression years, and the war years, when there wasn't much to buy in Coushatta, and it was hard to drive to Shreveport, the nearest city. As the Depression loosened its strangle-hold on us, the war, World War II, loomed closer and breathed down our necks, despite the fact that we didn't even have a clue there were enemy submarines right off the coast in the Gulf of Mexico. We knew our country was in a war that would determine what kind of world we would spend the rest of our lives in; so we celebrated when we could; we lived and loved and laughed; dreaming of an even better tomorrow.

There were inconveniences connected to wartime living, of course. Now everything was scarce: cars, gasoline, tires, and luxury items of all kinds. While the war soon began to put more money back into the economy, money, at least in our part of the country was still relatively scarce, and many foods and other consumer goods were rationed. With our country's entry into World War II all citizens were required to sacrifice for the war effort and were encouraged to go beyond what was required. We bought War Bonds and saved scrap iron and aluminum, and planted victory gardens. But these sacrifices didn't seem like burdens to us. They were a duty we gladly accepted when so many were sacrificing their lives.

Our family was richly blessed in having the things we really needed and the rest seemed much less important than it does today. We had a comfortable home, a loving community of friends, a vital church "family," and a fierce determination to help achieve our nation's goal of ridding the world of the evils of dictatorship and cruel atrocities of war. We had the hope of a lasting peace to look forward to when this terrible war was over.

The young men who were visiting us at Christmas knew that very soon they would be shipping overseas to join in the fighting; they just didn't know where to, or if they did they certainly didn't talk about it. We didn't talk about those things. All of us, young and old alike, realized that the war would soon be affecting us in more direct, more personal ways and on that Christmas night when we gathered around the piano to sing the familiar carols of Christmas, it was only natural to mix in a few of the current popular hits as well, such as *From Taps 'til Reveille, When the Lights Go On Again All over the World,* and *Don't Sit Under the Apple Tree with Anyone Else but Me.*

Right then, we were content to live in the moment, enjoying the good things the Good Lord had given us; the good times, the bright days, the celebrations. Christmas, birthdays, graduations, all took on new meaning as we lived every moment as it came and prayed earnestly for peace on earth and a brighter tomorrow. The best thing was being with people we loved.

The good people of our little town drew close together in our hearts as we wrote letters and sent packages to our service men, comforted the families whose loved ones had made the supreme sacrifice; those who were missing, or suffering in enemy prison camps. We tended our victory gardens, listened to the war news, and continued to make plans for the future...or at least, this is the way I remember it.

Chapter 9

High School Days

The Sun Goddesses

IT'S TEN O'CLOCK in the morning and I have my room all cleaned up, just like Momnee asked me to. It's so boring to have to do housework, but in the summer, especially in the mornings there's really not much else to do. I could read, I guess, but I've already read all Momnee's magazines, and the "Seventeen" and "Modern Screen" and "True Romances" at the Drug Store. Wait, is that the phone?

"I'll get it!" I have to be quick to beat Aunt Howard to it. I know she's hoping for a call from her "Cud'n Winnie," as she calls her. Old ladies are so funny on the phone. They must not have much to talk about.

"Hello." (Oh, good. It's Marcia on the other end. She's fifteen; two years older than me, and she has dozens of boyfriends; well several, to be exact. I hope I'll be popular like her someday, but that's not likely to happen.)

"Oh, hi! It's you. Nothin', really. Actually I'm bored to pieces. What are you doin'?

I've been hopin' you'd call . . ."

"Uh-huh. Oh, you're sun-bathin' again? Gosh, if I could get a tan like yours, I'd love to come and join you, but you KNOW what happens to me. Freckles by the millions . . . Oh, no, I don't think that would work . . . No. I don't think so . . . W-e-l-l, okay, maybe for just a few minutes. Yeah, maybe that would be okay. See you in a minute; soon as I get my suit on."

Marcia lives across the street, just two houses down. If I can just find the top to my bathing suit I can be there in five minutes. Where, oh, where . . . ? I didn't finish putting all my stuff up from 4-H camp; most of it had to go in the dirty clothes hamper. But I wouldn't of put my bathing suit in there.

"Aunt Howard!" I'm yelling now. "Have you seen the top to my bathing suit? It was with all the things I unpacked when I came back from 4-H Camp last Friday."

"Now how in the world am I supposed to keep up with you kids' stuff, when you can't even keep up with it your selves? It looks like to me you're old enough to at least keep your things put up. When I was your age, do you know what-all I had to do? I had to . . ."

"Never mind," I cut her off. "I found it. I'm going over to Marcia's for a while. I'll be back in time for dinner. Or maybe we'll just eat a sandwich over there."

"Well, what in the world are y'all gonna do in your bathing suits? There aren't any BOYS over there are there?" Aunt Howard sounds like she's not in a very good mood; it's a good thing she doesn't know Mercille's not at home, or she prob'ly wouldn't let me go.

"No, Aunt Howard, there aren't any boys in our plan; we don't even like old boys. We're just gonna take a quick little sun bath in the back yard. Just us; nobody else. We might play cards or something for a little while, too."

Aunt Howard doesn't look one bit pleased. "Edith Joy, you know you're gonna blister in that blazin' hot sun right here in the middle of the day. You *know*, with your fair skin…well, you know what's gonna happen. I think you'd better just stay here and help a little bit around the house this morning."

"Please, *please*, Aunt Howard. I'll sit under the pecan tree in the shade most of the time. I won't have to get in the sun at all. It's shady in the back yard. And anyhow, I already told Marcia I'm coming, and I don't want to disappoint her."

"I don't know what makes you so hard-headed, Edith Joy. You're just like your daddy sometimes. I guess if Marcia told you to go jump off the river bridge, you'd do it without batting an eye. I don't have time to stand here all mornin' arguing with you. If you get blistered it's just you and your mama for it. She lets you kids get away with way too much, if you ask me. But of course, nobody asks me." Aunt Howard's just shakin' her head as she goes back in the kitchen. I'm getting outta here now before she can change her mind. She doesn't seem to realize I'm going to be in High School this fall, and I'm old enough to start making more of my own decisions now. She still treats me like a baby.

"Hi, Joy! I'm sure glad you decided to come and sun bathe with me. We can spread the quilt out here, so your part can be mostly in the shade and mine in the sun."

Marcia's already smoothing baby oil on her arms and legs and her middle. "Here, gimme that oil and I'll slather it on your back for you." Marcia already has what I consider to be a beautiful golden tan, but it's not quite dark enough to suit her.

I plop down on my side of the quilt and strike a really glamorous pose, or I'm sure at least it *would* be if my bathing suit and I were just a tiny bit more glamorous. It's hard to be glamorous with white skin and stringy hair and freckles. We gossip for a while about who's claiming whom for boyfriends and girlfriends, and who's broken up with whom since school's now out for the summer. I'm lying on my stomach while we talk, not noticing that the sun has moved ever so slightly in its customary path, erasing my little spot of shade, and directing its blazing rays with full force on my arms and shoulders.

Right in the middle of a fascinating dialogue about the new basketball cheerleaders I'm startled as I suddenly realize what's happening to me and I begin crawling back toward the shade. I feel like my skin is frying in baby oil. This could be a disaster. I guess Momnee's right. She says I need to think things through a little more carefully.

"Wait, don't move yet," Marcia says. "I just thought of a brilliant idea. You really want a tan, don't you, Joy?" (If she only knew. Sometimes I lie awake at night picturing myself with a golden tan, wearing a white halter-top sundress, with my shoulders bared in all their golden splendor; my legs dark against the blinding white of the skirt and my painted toenails sticking out of white sandals.)

"Are you crazy?" I'm almost yelling now. "You *know* how much I want a tan, but for me it will never happen. I was destined to have freckles. I'm sure I'll have a whole new crop tomorrow. That's just the way it is. Fair skin is just not *fair*. I hate it! I don't even want to talk about it anymore," I pouted.

"But wait, listen to this: Don't give up." (It's *Marcia* who won't give up.) "I think maybe you've just been going about this in the wrong way," Marcia argues. "I have a theory that you haven't been staying in the sun *long* enough. Haven't you learned in Science about theories? It's when you believe something is true, but you don't know for sure, so you have to test it out to prove whether you're right or not. Now, if I'm right, all you need to do is stay in the sun long enough for your freckles to run together and then you'll have a tan. Doesn't that make sense? Oh, it would be so pretty. Your freckles are a nice gold color. Why don't we just test my theory right now?"

Gosh, it sounds tempting. It sounds reasonable, too, when you put it in scientific terms like that. "Maybe if I put lots of the baby oil on, it will help the freckles run together. That stuff is real slippery." I want so much to believe. "Do you really think it will work? But Marcia, what if it *doesn't* work? No, I don't think I'd better do it." (Oh ye of little faith)

"Well, it's your decision, Joy. Either you really want a tan, or you don't. Mother always says, 'You have to suffer to be beautiful.' I know I'd do anything to get a good tan if I didn't already have one. But, of course, it's up to you." She shook her head, turned over on the blanket and closed her eyes.

Could it be true that it's my own fault that I don't have a tan? If I don't mind frying in baby oil, can I really have a tan? Maybe it's worth a try. What could go wrong except that I might get a *ba-a-d* sunburn? Oh, well, it wouldn't be the first time, and so I take a deep breath.

"I think I'll try for the tan," I whisper in excitement, feeling adventurous and even a little hopeful as I smooth on more oil and settle on the quilt for another try. (Or would it be just another fry?) I might accumulate more freckles, but who's going to notice a few more freckles among so many?

It's beautiful weather, not too hot for late June, and soon we're both dozing. Minutes turn into an hour and who knows what might have happened if we hadn't been startled awake by the clatter-crash-bang of the garbage truck pulling up in the driveway. We grab for the quilt and towels, sling them over our half - bare bodies, and make a dive for the back porch. Just in time. Well, not *quite* in time. Marcia's tan has acquired a rosy glow, but the white skin of the "snow princess" has taken on a lobster hue, and there is a cry of pain as I feel the roughness of the towel against bare skin. So much for Marcia's theory.

A painful night and a few days later most of the burned skin has peeled off. Only two or three tactless people even mention that I seem to have a few more freckles than usual. There will be no white halter-top sundress for me this summer; or perhaps ever. I realize that my punishment is the result of my own stupidity. But only a clod like Fred Jr. would sing a song that includes the words: ". . . she's got freckles on her BUT—she is pretty . . ."

Teenagers – A New Species?

Yesterday, at the ripe old age of 84 I discovered while reading an article in a current Time magazine that the notion of the teen years as a distinct stage of life came into common acceptance and usage in this country right after the Great Depression, during the decade of the 1940's. That statement didn't come as any great surprise to me; I officially became a member of this group on October 5, 1942. Even though I've always been a "late-bloomer" I could tell even at age thirteen that life had suddenly become different. For one thing there were more choices to make and I began to have vague forebodings that my actions at this time in my existence could have a strong impact on my "future." Of course I didn't necessarily let that influence my behavior in a positive way because this "future" still lay in some distant happily-ever-after land but sometimes I did think about it with a bit of anxiety in the middle of the night.

One of the times I remember this happening was when I was invited to go with a bunch of my buddies to "get" some sugar cane down on the old river road, from some "unknown" landowner's field. We had met up at the Rec Center that evening and found nothing much going on there, so someone suggested this little adventure. I don't even remember whose idea it was, but before I had much time to think about it I found myself climbing into the back of a small cattle truck with six or eight of my friends on a dark October night, trusting our driver to get us safely and securely down a muddy dirt road to this generic patch of sugar cane. The fact that this was a place I didn't need to go, had no legal right to be in, and didn't really care to be in, didn't even enter my mind. I just wanted to be where my friends were. Besides, I was bored and looking for a little excitement.

Of course I had heard of teenagers stealing watermelons—and sugar cane—at night, but had never actually considered doing it myself; for one thing, I couldn't see the point; I liked watermelon, but it didn't really cost all that much. On the other hand, I did not have any use for sugar cane whatsoever; no desire at all to chew on the stuff; I'd tried it once and didn't care for the taste of the juice. Probably my friends didn't either; we just liked the idea of adventure, and doing crazy things together. When one of the girls asked, "Are we gonna get in trouble? Is it against the law to steal sugar cane?" one of the boys said, "aw, stealin' sugar cane ain't like real stealin', it's more like liftin'. I bet y'all have all lifted stuff before haven't ya?" Nobody answered. So, of course, we were shortly on our way to rediscover the thrill of illicit adventure.

Soon our driver slowed the vehicle to a crawl and then pulled off the muddy road, crossed a small ditch and eased the truck right up into the edge of the cane rows, hoping it would be completely hidden on this moonless night. We began looking for a place that was not too muddy, to jump out of the truck. It was at that point that I realized this whole thing might be a big mistake, but it was too late to turn back now. Someone gave me a little push and I toppled over the edge of the back-end of that truck and landed with a big squish in the mud. I could hear my precious new white loafers make a sucking sound as they sploshed completely out of sight with me still in them.

Suddenly a shot rang out of nowhere, and an angry voice yelled, "Get outta my blankety-blank cane field the same way ya got in, and dontcha *ever* come back if ya know what's good for ya! Blankety- blank crazy kids!" This unexpected explosion was followed by mass confusion as we scrambled wildly, climbing all over one another getting back into the truck as our terrified driver started the engine, sailed across the ditch and frantically found his way back onto that dirt road without anyone saying a word. It was a quiet ride all the way back into town. Only then was I able to properly grieve for my new white loafers. I had to leave them behind in the mud, of course —a small price to pay for our successful escape—but I did love them so much, even though they were so impractical. (I think that's why I loved them.) Oh, well! So much for wild adventure in our rural Eden called Red River Parish.

As I remember, this was only the first of several wild, hard to explain escapades that I participated in, some of them willingly and all of them unthinkingly, during my teen years. We were very lucky not to have paid a steep price for such thoughtless and unacceptable behavior: just having a little fun at someone else's expense. Compared with many of the ways that some bored and/or defiant teenagers amuse themselves today, this episode probably doesn't even deserve mentioning. I think the only reason I even remember it is that it was not characteristic behavior for the group that I ran with. We were mostly well-behaved, church-going kids whose parents trusted us. We just sometimes felt the need for pushing the limits; testing to see how far we could go without getting caught; or maybe just trying to forget parental restraints for a while and making our own rules.

Once in a while I did remember my childhood experience of "white-collar crime" in Miss Tressie's fifth grade with some remorse, and wondered if my more recent surrenders to temptation were as bad as that time long ago when we planned together and carried out our dastardly plot to cheat on that test. Probably not, because these more recent sins were not premeditated. They just sort of happened. I do know that I learned a lesson, because I never cheated again; ever.

I am thankful to God that we never had to pay the price of tragic consequences for any of our crazy, unthinking teenage pranks. My brother-in-law, Archie Worsham, who was a teacher, coach and school principal, and father to three boys, has often declared that it is just by the grace of God that any teenager survives to the age of adulthood, and I agree. But he also asserts that most of them do survive, not because of what we parents do, but in spite of everything we do. Over the years I have suspected that this situation has only changed by degree. Happily, his children and mine have grown to be adults.

I remember from a college graduate level course in Adolescent Psychology that "for adolescents to become well adjusted, fully functioning adults, children need to receive from their parents a balanced amount of both LOVE and DISCIPLINE." I don't remember who the psychologist was who said that but from my own experience as a teacher and a parent I also agree with that statement, and I'm sure it is as true today as it was then.

Slam Books – Fad of the 40's?

It's eight o'clock on a cool October morning; almost time for the bell to ring for classes to start at Coushatta High School. Why in the world are all those girls huddled up in one corner over there? Looks like there's something kind of unusual going on—or is it just my imagination? I don't know what makes me think so, but I think they're talking about something pretty exciting and it must be kind of secret, too; kind of "hush-hush," I guess you might say. None of my bunch are over there. I don't want to get myself into any kind of trouble, but my curiosity is about to kill me now. Maybe if I just walk over a little closer I can hear enough to figure out what's going on.

It seems to be mostly 10th graders, and I don't want them to think I'm trying to stick my nose into something that's none of my business. As I ease over closer I can see Laura Jean walking that way; I'll bet she's curious, too. Yeah, she's headed that way for sure. Nobody ever gets mad at her; students and teachers all seem to like her. Yeah, I think I'll just ease over there with her.

As I get closer I can see that they've got their heads in some kind of notebook. When they realize we're about to join the group, somebody slaps the book shut real quick and they begin walking away. Now I can see that Marcia is a part of the group, so I feel better now. I know she'll tell me what it's all about. I'll ask her about it later, but I'd better phone her this afternoon after school. I don't

want anybody to hear us talking about it here at school.
If we had a real live Nancy Drew in our group she'd find
out the answer to this mystery. I wish Marcia still lived
in our old neighborhood, so I could go to her house and
talk with her but I know she'll tell me what it's all about
because she has always been one of my best friends, even
though she's two years older than me.

I did remember to phone Marcia, right after school,
and ask her about the little gathering that I saw taking
place in the outdoor area called the "girls' court" located
in the covered portico between the auditorium and the
girls' restrooms. At first she couldn't figure out what I was
talking about, but then when I mentioned the names of
some of the girls who were in the group, and as soon as
I said the word "notebook," she lowered her voice a little
and said "oh, yes, now I know what you're talking about.
I'll try to tell you what I can about it, but it's a little hard
to explain." She went on to try to describe the notebook
I had mentioned, then changed her mind and suggested
that I meet her before school the next morning in that
same area, so I could see for myself what it was all about.
She seemed hesitant to say anything more, so I changed
the subject.

The next morning I got to school a little earlier than
usual and headed straight for the "girls' court." Marcia
arrived just a few minutes later. She asked me to stay with
her when her group began to gather and to watch for
notebooks in the hands of some of the girls. I stayed and
joined in the general morning greetings and small talk and
then pretty soon one of the girls pulled out a notebook
similar to the one I had seen yesterday. When she opened

it and I managed to squeeze in close enough to figure out what the contents of the page contained, I almost wished I hadn't allowed my curiosity to pull me into this situation. There didn't seem to be any way to withdraw from it gracefully now. Soon my eyes were drawn to the contents like a magnet.

As I looked more closely it reminded me of a plain old autograph book, but then I saw clearly the name of one of the tenth grade girls at the top of the page in big letters. It was what was written underneath that really caught my attention. It said something like, "I heard you want to date BJA but he thinks you're ugly." There were all kinds of catty little sayings, many of them printed and most of them without signatures but instead little nick-names like "U NO HOO", or "Guess Who?" Some people wrote nice comments, like "cute girl" but most of them were sarcastic, some meant to be funny and some just plain mean. Marcia whispered to me, "they're called Slam Books," as we headed for the back entrance.

As the school year went by I had plenty of opportunities to examine slam books more closely, as they became quite a fad for a while. As I remember there were some informal "rules" that went with the activity; (it became almost like a club.) Things like: you could only write comments under girls' names if you allowed your name to be put in the book for others to comment on. I found out the hard way that it could be very hurtful to open a slam book and see a comment under your name like, "she stinks." You know it's crazy to take something like that seriously, but you find yourself wondering who feels that way about you, and why. It would be even worse if the comment was something like, "she might be pretty if she didn't have freckles." I used to wonder why none of the teachers knew this was going on, or if they did, why they didn't do something about it.

2017 Looking Back - Bullying

Today it is called "bullying" or cyber-bullying, and everyone knows how tragic the consequences can be. I don't think the teens of my day took it to the extremes that some do today, and we certainly didn't have the tech devices that make it so easy now to escalate and cause serious damage. However, memories like this make me realize how important it is to teach our children to be kind. And to remember that the best way to teach is by example.

Serving Their Country – And Ours

I have thought many times over the years how different my teen years would have been if my girlfriends and I had not had the experience of getting to know a group of young men we came to think of as "our soldier boys" or "our GIs". Those young men were in their late teens and early twenties and were in the Signal Corps, stationed at Camp Beauregard, near Alexandria, LA, but they were temporarily camped at our local fairgrounds in Coushatta for about six months. In a small town like Coushatta there was nothing for them to do in their free time. No bars, no nightclubs, no USO of course.

There was not much for the young people of the community to do, either, except that our parents, with the help of the Town had recently acquired an old store building a couple of blocks from the school, and across from the Parish Courthouse, which they turned into a recreation center for our use during after-school hours. It was the perfect place for us teens to congregate. There were two large rooms; one with a Jukebox and a dance floor, and the other with a pool table, ping pong table, and an area for booths, tables and snacks. A group of mothers volunteered as chaperones; it was a safe place for us to be with our friends and to stay out of trouble. I suppose we could even have used it as a place to study, but I don't remember that ever happening.

Not long after the military moved into town they discovered our little teen haven and they were welcomed warmly; there was no alcohol allowed, but that didn't

High School friends and our GIs

discourage them. It surely didn't keep them away. Ours was a "dry municipality," anyhow. This new situation (including GIs in our teen center activities) didn't seem to bother the high school boys, either. They continued to frequent the place and put up with the competition. Most of them were too busy with basketball practice to spend much time at the "Rec" anyhow, and of course we girls had no objections to a whole new crop of nice and nice-looking young men who seemed to know all the new dance steps and were more than willing to teach them to us. The community was very welcoming; it was our patriotic duty to do what we could to make our military men feel welcome in our community. They were our heroes.

As soon as school was out for summer vacation my friends and I began going out to the fairgrounds on Sunday afternoons to watch the ball games our GI boyfriends were playing. Sometimes we even dared to go down by the

Watching the games

Our own private "beach"

river and create our own private beach and wade in the river when the water got low enough. We discovered that the biggest difference between dating GIs and the local boys we had known all our lives was that we didn't have to worry about any kind of sexual misbehavior or pushiness from the GIs. They were fine young men, but they probably had been warned that any such behavior would not be tolerated. The two young men I spent most of my time with were Gene Smith from Marietta, GA and Jack Mackenroth from Pittsburgh, PA. They were both in their late teens and knew they would be going overseas soon. Gene visited in our home at Christmas and went on later to Japan. I wrote to both boys for a while after they went overseas and I went on to college. I never had any contact with them after they got out of service, but it was great fun for me and my friends while it lasted. Meanwhile, I plunged ahead with my school activities and plans for high school graduation and college.

"Miss Smarty" – Movie Queen for a Day

"Momnee!" I almost yell into my mother's office phone. "Guess what happened at school today. Oh, well, I'll just tell you; you'd *never* guess. Mrs. Smith gave out the parts for the senior play and I'm going to be a movie star!... No, it's not the leading part; I'll tell you all about it when you get home ... I'm sorry, I just had to call 'cause I couldn't wait to tell you. Will you be home pretty soon? ... Oh, okay ... Yeah, I *am* excited and no, I'm *not* disappointed that I didn't get the lead. This is just as good; maybe even better ... Okay, I'll tell you all about it then. Bye." I hang up the phone and run straight to my room.

I'm grinning all over as I fling myself onto the bed with a shriek of pure delight. What I really want to do is jump up and down on the bed like when I was a little kid. How did I ever get so lucky? The name of the play is "Miss Smarty," and I'm gonna get to play the part of Miss Smarty herself, a "glamorous movie star." That's the way it describes her right here in the playbook. At first

I thought it had to be a mistake, because there are several girls in the senior class who are lots more glamorous than me, but I checked and it isn't a mistake. It's true.

I guess maybe the reason I'm so excited about this is that one of my favorite games when I was a little girl was pretending to be a movie star, so it's kind of like a dream come true. I've always liked being in plays; even the ones we used to make up and present on our backyard "stage" when we lived in "The Little House" on Twitchell Street. I liked being in the school plays, too. I was an angel in the Christmas pageant in Second Grade, and Duchess of the May Fete in Fourth Grade.

The best play I was ever in, though, was when I was ten going on eleven and played the part of a 9-year old girl in the American Legion fund-raiser. At first the director didn't want to let me be in it because she thought I was too young and wouldn't be able to memorize all the lines and sing the songs. My mother was in the play, too, and she explained that I was almost eleven, just small for my age. She promised I would learn all my lines and I turned out to be a pretty good actor. I played the part of a bratty little girl and that part fit me just right.

I memorized just about the whole play, and even gave the grown-up actors prompts when they forgot their lines, or missed a cue. That probably wasn't a good idea. Oh, well, I learned something from that experience. Being in that play was a lot of fun; it was a musical and we sang lots of songs. I even got to sing a solo. It was kind of a dumb song, but I guess it fit me pretty well. The name of it was "Your Time's Coming." I still remember some of the words:

"Your time's coming, your time's coming by and by
Every time I hear those words it almost makes me cry.
I hope I can find a way to grow up big like you some day,
But in the meantime please don't say,
Your time's coming by and by."

Now I'm singing at the top of my lungs while I'm thinking about what it's like being on the stage. Even though it's just a memory from long ago I can still feel that tingle that comes from hearing the audience laugh and clap and cheer, as they enjoy the performance.

I'm glad the beautiful star of that long ago play isn't in our senior class today. Sarah Helene Holley, with the long, wavy black hair, and a perfect complexion like the girls in the Camay soap ads - most beautiful girl I've ever seen; she'd be the perfect "Miss Smarty." I'd be sitting home doing geometry homework today while she's telling somebody how great it is to be a movie star in the senior play.

And now, my sister, Alexa, walks in just in time to miss my vocal solo; I guess she heard it out in the hall, though, because she's standing there giving me "that look." Which always gets my attention even though she's younger than me; she can be intimidating at times.

"What are you doing lying up there in the bed singing in the middle of the afternoon?" She asks. "You didn't get into Aunt Howard's fruitcake wine, did you? I'm gonna tell on you."

"Ha-ha, you're so-o-o funny! Not that it's any of your business, but I'm just lying here happily thinking about the senior play," I toss back at her in my smart-aleck kind of way; I can be sarcastic when I need to. I'm trying to have a smug look on my face but as usual my younger sister is not the least bit impressed.

"What's so '*happily*' about the senior play?" she asks; she can be kind of a smart-aleck, too, when she wants to. We really like each other, but I'm just a little more mature than she is, so we tend to get in these silly arguments.

"Well, can't a person be permitted to be happy in their own home?" (I'm getting a little tired of all this ridiculous small talk.) "I'm just kidding. Guess what? The name of our senior play is 'Miss Smarty,' and I, your very own sister—am Miss Smarty!" I gush.

"No, kidding? I could have told you that. You used to hate it when Aunt Howard called you that." And we both burst out laughing.

"Hi, you girls, I'm home." Momnee says to us with a big smile as she pushes the front door open and joins us in our bedroom, giving each of us a little hug.

"Tell her! Tell her the news about the play!" Almost before Alexa gets the words out she claps her hands over her mouth and looks sheepishly at me with those big, beautiful brown eyes of hers. (Why couldn't I have gotten those eyes instead of her? And she got the curly hair, too. It's just not fair!)

"Don't worry," I reassure Alexa, "I wasn't trying to surprise Momnee. I already called her at the office to tell her because I couldn't wait for her to get home."

"You called her at the *office*? I thought that was a no-no." Alexa pretends to be horrified. (She does it, too, sometimes.)

Momnee grabs me then in a big hug, and says, "Congratulations!" I know she would probably be prouder of me if

I had gotten the leading role. When she was at Louisiana State Normal College she was in lots of plays; in the Davis Players, the college drama group, too. Alexa and I used to get out her old Potpourris (the college yearbooks) and look at her pictures in the plays she starred in. She looked so pretty on the stage. She *always* looks pretty to me.

"Momnee, I'm really okay with the role I got. It's not the lead role, but it'll be fun, I think. Miss Smarty is a movie star who is just so full of her own importance. She's a pretty ridiculous character, trying to be more sophisticated and worldly wise than she actually is. But she's not a mean person and in the last act you end up liking her. The lead role is just a sweet, pretty young girl without any eccentric personality traits.

Suddenly I start thinking about that song I sang in the long ago American Legion play:

. . . Your time's coming, your time's coming by and by . . . and it almost seems that the lines of that song are beginning to come true for me now. I'm feeling pretty grown up, and suddenly it's happening way too fast. I like it, but it's kinda scary, too. Beginning to think about the future; about college, and even about what will happen *after* college. That's probably not even normal for people my age. But right now all I can think about is the play. This is the most exciting thing that's happened to me in a long time.

We have a week to study our lines and then we begin play practice every day after school. It's exciting, but some of it is plain hard work. Some of the cast members are beginning to grumble and complain a little, especially the boys, but I love it. I'm lucky, having such an interesting role, but not so many lines as the main characters; I kinda have the best of both worlds. We do a lot of clowning around backstage and almost drive Mrs. Smith crazy some days but we have fun working together and I think we're getting to know each other in a new way. Many of us have known each other since first grade, but now we're working on something we have in common that we didn't have before. We all want this to be a good play; the best senior play ever. This is *our* senior play. We're the great class of '46, by golly!

Since I'm playing the part of a glamorous movie star I have to have glamorous clothes, right? And since there are no glamorous clothes in my closet—or anywhere in Coushatta—that means a shopping trip to Shreveport, right? It's hard for me to get very excited about this part because I know we'll be doing our shopping at a boring place like Sears or J.C.Penney's like we always do. How much glamour can you find there? Might as well just drag out the old Montgomery Ward catalog, or go to the Goodwill store. If I get lucky maybe Momnee will take me to one of the cheap-but-grown-up places like Lerner's. The War's over, but I know our budget can't survive a trip to one of the more expensive shops; I need a dressy suit, blouse, hat, shoes; the works!

We're on our way to the big city and I'm daydreaming about the play as we cross the Shreveport-Bossier Bridge. Even though I'm a senior about to graduate from high school, I am 16 years old but my mother still won't let me drive anywhere except in Coushatta. I hate to admit it, even to myself, but I think she's right about that. I'm glad she's driving today because I'm not really confident enough, especially in a city. I'm glad she's driving and now I'm actually excited about this trip in spite of our budget restrictions. Momnee hasn't even mentioned the word, "budget" once, which I take as a good sign, and I'm beginning to rouse a little as she says, "Wake up, 'Miss Smarty,' we're almost there. Watch for a parking spot in one of the lots as we get closer to Selbers. They should have plenty of choices. Do you have any ideas about what you're looking for?"

Momnee sounds real cheerful and almost as chummy as one of my girlfriends. Suddenly I realize what she just said! Or maybe I'm still dreaming. "Did you say Selbers'?" I ask in a sort of casual manner, hoping it isn't a dream, but if so, that I won't wake up. That's where my friend, Ruth Lester, buys her clothes: it's too expensive for us.

"Yep," Momnee answers. "I thought we could start our search there. They usually have lots of choices in the latest styles. But what about your ideas, Joy?"

"I like some of the new styles they're showing in 'Seventeen Magazine' and other fashion magazines they have at the drug store. I'm hoping to find something similar to those at the stores here."

"Sounds like you've been doing your homework, 'Miss Smarty.' Good for you! That should make our shopping easier. I hope you won't be terribly disappointed if we can't find exactly what you have in mind. What about colors?"

"I'm not sure. I just know that I want some green somewhere in the picture. I always get compliments when I wear green. But it will have to be just the right shade."

"Better start looking for that parking spot," Momnee reminds me, as she turns off of Texas Street. "You're right about the color. Green is one of your best colors. Red-heads can't go wrong wearing green, especially if it's just the right shade."

What a fun day! I tried on three suits before I found the one that was exactly right. Momnee liked it too, but I didn't let that discourage me from buying it. Actually she has pretty good taste. The suit fits me perfectly; it's a silvery shade of gray, with a fine, window-pane pattern in deep green. The hat I chose was gray and I found a silky blouse that matched the green in the suit. But the shoes are the best of all! They're from Goldring's! They're deep green with three-inch heels and made of dyed Cobra skin; absolutely perfect with the rest of the outfit, and they'll be great to take to college with me.

I've never had so much money spent on me at one time in my whole life, except maybe when I had my tonsils out when I was four. Now I'll be able to walk out on the stage and act like a real movie star because I know a little of what it feels like to be a star.

Senior Play

As the big night draws near, we decide to celebrate by painting our names on the wall behind the stage curtain. Some of the boys argue for putting them in a more prominent place but Francez Sigler warns us we might get in trouble if we do that. She oughta know, cause her dad, Mr. A.L. Sigler is Superintendent of Schools. We decided it would be more fun to hide them so we'll be the only people who know they're there until, maybe sometime in the far distant future someone will find our handiwork and think, "My, what nice names! That must have been a great play; a great class, that class of 1946! I wish I could have seen their play."

Looking Back

There was something about being a senior, being in the play, going to the Junior-Senior Banquet; no words could describe that experience. It felt like breaking out into the real world; the big world outside the school walls; ready at last for new things; new experiences, going places and seeing things I'd never experienced before. My life was beginning to unfold before me and I embraced the feeling with confidence. "Look out world, here I come!" Still, something seemed to be tugging at my coat tails, whispering, "The scary part will come later." I was right but it was not until much later. The optimism and self-confidence remained with me, and in time and with God's grace which my mother with her Wesleyan background instilled in me, I had the faith to see me through. But of course there were some bumps along the way.

Graduation is Only the Beginning

The last part of my senior year in High School, after the thrill of the Senior Play was over, there were really only two things on my mind. For the entire month of May I was caught up in the excitement of the graduation and all the hustle and bustle that went with it; the presents, the parties; but at the same time, *always* in the back of my mind, thoughts of college and plans and preparation for this new venture so imminent and so important were constantly competing for my time and attention.

My friend Edris and I stayed busy the rest of the school year; as soon as we finished our plans and preparations for entering Northwestern State, the graduation parties began. I invited the class to a Latin American supper-dance in our back yard. It was really just a regular dance; no rhumbas or tangos but I made the invitations, which had a colorful Carmen Miranda look-alike that I drew, myself, on the front and we played some Latin music and drank some pretend Margaritas.

We went to another really fun party which was also a dance at the Magnolia Club House at Harmon. It was given by some of the new students who came to CHS after the Grand Bayou School had to close after the flood in April of 1945. I had a date for that party with Eugene Johnson, whose dad was principal of the Grand Bayou School. The most exciting thing about that night for me was the ride home. We were a carload of teens. There was a gardenia bush at the clubhouse that was in full bloom. We picked about a hundred blooms and filled the car with them, then partially rolled down the car windows so that the blooms began blowing all over the inside of the car. It smelled heavenly in that car; I feel sure we were driving way too fast, but it was an unusually refreshing ride.

The graduation ceremony itself would have been nicer except for one thing that really bothered me. A couple of weeks before graduation our class sponsor gave me the news that I was valedictorian and that meant that I would be giving the Valedictory Address. Well, in the first place I was quite surprised, but then I realized that this would probably never have happened except that both Ira Campbell, Jr. and Bert Stephens went away to Wentworth Academy for their last two years in high school and weren't even in the running.

The second surprise was that when I was given this news I was also handed a manuscript and told that this was the speech I was to give. My first reaction to this situation was shock that I'd been listening to all these valedictorians give speeches all these years and thinking they were so smart. My *next* reaction was just a wee bit of anger to think that these teachers didn't think we were smart enough to write our own valedictory speeches.

My third and last reaction was, of course, a sigh of relief. No more anger, just a bit of disappointment. I did learn something from the experience, though. I have graduated twice since that first time, and never again went into it with unrealistic expectations. I have to admit that I did have a little resentment and even a bit of guilt to realize that I was misleading a rather large crowd of listeners to think that the ideas I was expressing were my own. I later understood that famous people all the way up the ladder to the president do it all the time and think nothing of it. Or do they? They have speech-writers, but they also have veto power. I finally had the presence of mind to read over "my" speech and found that it was so innocuous there was nothing I could actually disagree with. Problem solved.

Looking Back

All of us have experienced defining moments in our lives; moments that brought strong feelings we will never forget along with a feeling that life will never be quite the same again. The first time that happened to me was when I was a child in the 1940's and watched two planes crash together, burst into flames, and plunge like wounded birds onto the riverbank during the war "Maneuvers" just prior to US entry into World War II. I had been told that these were "War Games" but I knew that what I saw that day was no game! It was real life. And death. And I was guessing that life would never be the same. I had a little peep into adulthood that day.

So many of us had similar feelings when we heard about the Japanese attack on Pearl Harbor, December 7, 1941, or as we watched on TV as terrorists attacked the World Trade Center in New York City on September 11, 2001. We live in our own safe little world and then suddenly something happens that we can't deny. Some sudden loss or disappointment, and our lives change. Not all of our defining moments are bad, of course; sometimes they bring great love, joy and excitement into our lives. But even the good ones are accompanied by that feeling that life will never be quite the same again. A good example of that is when our first child is born.

When it comes to defining moments, compared with the events I have just recalled, High School graduation is not even worth mentioning, but I do still remember some of the thoughts and feelings I had about the future. About leaving home and family, being on my own, having new experiences. The *feelings* were not as strong as the thoughts and dreams. And they were good ones. There was a little fear but my naïve optimism more than made up for that; there was a tiny bit of underlying sadness at leaving home and family, but my callow enthusiasm took care of that.

Perhaps one of the most important things I learned from my experience as a student is that graduation from any educational institution at any level of attainment is really only another beginning.

Coushatta High School

CHAPTER 10

College Days at NSC

Freshman (Again)

AFTER GRADUATING from Coushatta High School in May, I began my college studies at Northwestern State College, Natchitoches, Louisiana in June. The year was 1946 and the war was over; I was sixteen years old and dying to leave home and go away to college. I was happy and excited at the idea of being on my own even though I would only be thirty miles away in the lovely historic town of Natchitoches, just a short bus ride away from my home in Coushatta. Going to college at last!

There had never been any question about my going to college; not even a question about what college it would be. I would go to Northwestern State because that was where my mother graduated twenty years earlier, and she was my role model. Besides, several of my friends were planning to go to NSC. I was not worried about missing family, friends, or the little town of Coushatta where I had lived all my life. I was ready and eager to be out on my own. I couldn't wait until Fall Semester, but decided to start in the summer so I would have a head start. Rushing out to meet life, with all it would have to offer, or all it would have to throw at me, the original tabula rasa, I was on my way to somewhere without a backward glance. At sixteen, after all, there's not much to look back at.

My friend, Edris and I spent much of our spare time during the last half of our senior year in high school planning for this momentous transition to adult life; REAL life. During sixth period study hall we passed notes back and forth with questions such as: Have you sent in your registration forms yet? Have you decided on a major? Should we ask for a room on first or second floor in Audubon Hall? (Our pick of the freshman dorms). We were planning to room together so we needed to get these minor details out of the way so we could get down to the important issues, such as social activities and the "right" clothes for those social activities, and whether to go through sorority rush in the fall.

We agreed that we needed only a few new clothes for the summer term. Major clothing purchases would be made later, in time for the important Fall Semester with football games, sorority rush parties and formal dances. Since both of us were on limited budgets, dumb as we were we still had sense enough to know we'd have to skimp and save when and wherever we could. The Depression mentality was a part of the recent past that still reared its ugly head at times, in many ways but especially in the form of parental expectations and controls concerning spending.

My family's financial outlook was improving. Daddy's grocery store was beginning to prosper now that wartime food shortages and rationing were ended. I was aware, however, that he had borrowed money to buy the business and that my three younger siblings deserved an education as much as I did. I had some scholarship money but it would not even cover essentials; certainly not luxuries. Edris's family was in about the same kind of financial situation that my family was. None of this dampened our spirits the least bit. We would simply have to be creative and plan well; which is what we did in our own unsophisticated way.

We decided that homemade clothes could be one answer to our problem. Edris's mother sewed beautifully and the lady who always made my formal dresses for piano recitals and school dances sewed well enough and her prices were reasonable; and so it was decided. We knew that our old high school outfits would have to do for wearing to classes. After all, they would be new to the Northwestern campus; but we both loved to dance so of course we needed full skirts and ruffled peasant blouses to wear for jitterbugging at the field house to the sounds of the jukebox in the evenings. We also needed new bathing suits to wear for the P.E. swimming class that all freshmen were required to take.

We began sketching ideas for our new clothes, passing them back and forth during study hall under the watchful and suspicious eye of Mrs. Juanita Smith, our highly competent English teacher, who wore very thick glasses but still couldn't see well, and was probably surprised at how studious we were turning out to be now that we were almost ready to leave for the big leagues.

We had an inspiration for another way to save money. We took our sketches down to L. P. Stephens & Co., or, as everyone called it, "the big store" and pored over the thick McCalls and Simplicity pattern books until we found patterns that we both liked and then purchased one pattern in each design and shared them. We were careful to buy materials that were not alike in color or design so we wouldn't look like the Bobbsey twins or something. We were happily surprised to find that there were even patterns for bathing suits, and the new synthetic materials such as nylon and acrylics worked just fine but we had a little trouble persuading our seamstresses to tackle that job. The results, however, were surprisingly more than satisfactory.

When the day for the big move finally arrived Edris and I crammed our belongings into the trunk and back seat of my family's car, a 1942 Plymouth, which was the last model Plymouth made before the United States declared war on the Japanese after the attack on Pearl Harbor; one of the last new cars sold in Coushatta until after the war. Cars were not driven as many miles during the war years, because of gasoline rationing, so our car looked quite new compared to most cars on the road at the time. We felt pretty good about ourselves, in spite of homemade clothes.

Momnee drove us to Natchitoches, to the NSC campus; almost none of the students had their own cars on campus. We parked in front of Audubon Hall, one of two freshman women's dorms on the campus. She began helping us unload bags, trunks and boxes; not very stylish luggage, but much like the bags we saw being unloaded by other parents from other cars, some of them much older and road-weary than ours. Yes, we felt confident and optimistic. We had arrived!

We soon noticed a group of young men shuffling around on the sidewalk with hands in pockets. Some had baseball caps covering their shaved heads; caps with letters that spelled out the owners' new freshman nicknames: "Dog Adams", "Dog Johnson" and "Dog Whatever." Most of them looked self-conscious and uncomfortable under our amused scrutiny but one of the group, a tall, muscular, handsome young man snapped to attention and confidently loped over to our car grinning broadly.

"'Scuse me, ma'am, Dog Harris at your service," he addressed Momnee but he was looking at Edris and me. "I'll be happy to handle those bags for you. They look pretty heavy." The group on the sidewalk laughed, then cheered, "Way to go, Dog! You learn fast. One of these days you're gonna make the Demons proud. Might even end up Student Body President." As the ad hoc cheering squad began to disperse, Dog Harris, ignoring the good-natured ribbing, grabbed a bag in each hand and raced up the steps to Audubon Hall. He set the bags down, flung the door wide open and yelled at the top of his lungs, "Man in the hall!"

Edris and I looked at each other astounded, trying unsuccessfully to suppress giggles that inevitably rose to the surface. Momnee gave us a disapproving look but we could see that she was hiding a smile, too. We suspected that this was not the first time "Dog Harris" had been through this routine. This was just part of the fraternity razzing that freshman boys go through; I thought it was silly and could actually be cruel and demeaning, when they did things like shaving the boys' heads, and whipping them with belts. Sometimes I'm really glad I'm a girl when I see things like that. I think we have a little more sense than boys do.

"What an interesting encounter. I'm enjoying college life already. I think it's a shame, though, the way the upperclassmen treat those poor freshman boys," I said when I recovered my composure. "Dogs," Edris reminded me, and we looked at each other again, and agreed that our enthusiastic Sir Galahad was also "cute." Momnee commented that she hoped all the boys at NSC were as nice and helpful as Dog Harris. We all wished we knew his first name and I thought to myself that I would try to find out soon.

When the "Dog" returned after insisting on delivering all of our heavy bags to room 108, he was whistling cheerfully. We thanked him and even offered a tip, which he refused. "No, ma'am, I wouldn't think of taking y'alls money. As a matter of fact, I should be thanking y'all. You ladies just saved me from a fate worse than death. I was set up to be the main attraction at a little hazing activity. What a shame you ladies in distress came along and caused me to miss it. Oh, well, I'm sure I'll have another opportunity soon enough. Bye, now. Maybe I'll see you in the registration lines!" We certainly hoped so.

Looking Back Much Later After College Graduation

Freshman hazing and fraternity hazing actually got worse before it got better. And it finally disappeared, or at least it was outlawed, on college and university campuses. But only after there were some incidents which resulted in much-publicized tragedies. If it still happens today, in the twenty-first century, you don't hear much about it.

Students with some seniority thought it was a lot of fun in earlier days. But, I suppose we finally learned that some fun is just not worth the consequences. The awful, sometimes irreversible, consequences.

It seems to me that the process of civilization is, more times than not, an evolutionary one. This is sad, in a way, because evolution is never a quick fix. It can take a long time to correct problems, unless you prefer a revolution. But I do think that we are learning. We are learning to cooperate with our creator in gradually becoming a more civilized society. And so, I have hope and faith that one day, eventually, the world will become a less violent, and a kinder place for everyone.

Looking Back Again – 2017

I am sorry to say that I picked up the morning newspaper recently and discovered that freshman hazing has reared its ugly head once again. This time at Louisiana State University in Baton Rouge. The incident led to the tragic death of a young man who was forced to drink a lethal amount of alcohol during a fraternity initiation ritual. And lead to the arrest of 10 fraternity members. The tragedies have not ended after all. When will we ever learn?

Home For Christmas – 1946

Edris and I spent one brief year together on the first floor of Audubon Hall at NSC. We had good times and learned to love and appreciate our other roommate, Margery, who was a serious student and worked in the Dining Hall. We also loved and respected our housemother, Mrs. David, who was kind, fair and STRICT. She ran a tight ship. We found out what *could* happen when one of our fellow residents, who happened to be the niece of Dr. Gibson, then President of the College, decided to test the house rules.

One Saturday night "Betty" and two of her friends went out for a night on the town, to the Triangle Club, which was off limits to NSC students. Her friends attempted to smuggle her back into the Dorm in a state of inebriation—actually that is too mild a description; she was so drunk they had to carry her in feet first—at the very moment when the curfew bell rang. The attempt could never have succeeded; not a one of them was in any condition to carry out such a delicate mission. They were no match for Mrs. David, even if they had all been stone-cold sober but when one of them tried to sign in for "Betty" their fate was sealed.

We never saw "Betty" again. No, they didn't execute her. The "powers that be" including her Uncle President simply sent her on her way back to her home state of Oklahoma "before she even sobered up good;" or so the rumors had it. It was sad, really. She didn't make it until Christmas, even with her uncle being president of the college; that's how strict they were at NSC back in those days; and how fair and swift judgment came down; especially in Mrs. David's Audubon Hall.

The fall days had flown by, filled with football games, rush parties, sorority meetings, oh, yes, and classes and studying, too. Christmas was only a short time away, and everyone had big plans. Edris couldn't wait to see her boyfriend, Shorty, who had already gone to work, out in the big world called "real life." I was eager to see my boyfriend, Sam, who was at Centenary College. I would be going with his parents to watch him play in a Centenary basketball game during the holidays.

"Let's plan some kind of Christmas get-together, Edris," I said, as she burst through the door and dumped jacket and books on her bed. "If we wait till we get home I'm afraid we just won't do it, and our boyfriends haven't even had a chance to meet."

She took off her shoes and propped her feet on top of the books; she seemed to be thinking hard about it. "You know, Joy, Shorty has so little time off at Christmas, I will probably be spending most, if not all of my time with him," she replied. I know now that she was trying to tell me something but I was just not listening.

"But, you *know* I meant to include him, too; and Sam and all our other old CHS friends that are available. So now; you don't have any excuses. We can have it at my house; I know Momnee won't mind. How about it? I'll do all the preparation so you two lovebirds can spend all your time on other things; so now; how about it?"

Edris sounded apologetic when she tried to make me understand. "You know how much I enjoy being with you and the others, but things are different. Shorty is the most important person in my life now; we're planning to be married. I have a feeling he will give me the engagement ring at Christmas. We have lots of planning to do; and we need some time to just be together."

"Edris!" I almost screamed. "Promise me you won't do anything foolish like dropping out of school after Christmas to get married. You know you're too young for that. You're just barely seventeen. I mean, I'm happy for you and all that, but you're not much older than I am; and I know I'm too young."

"Hey, is this the same girl who told me I didn't have a right to nag just because we were going to be roommates? And now you're trying to tell me how to run my life?" Edris was showing me a spunky side of her that I had not seen before. She was right, of course. I had assumed things would go on as they were for at least a little while longer, but I had guessed things were getting pretty serious with her and Shorty.

"How do your parents feel about all this? Do they even know about it?" I hoped this was not going to break their hearts. I couldn't even imagine breaking news like this to my parents. I had not even considered having a choice in a decision like this.

"Of course they know about it. They're happy and excited for me. They have always liked Shorty and I think they have known for a long time that we would get married someday. I don't understand your attitude." Tears were beginning to fill Edris' eyes.

It was then that I recognized how selfish I had been. I was thinking about myself, not Edris and Shorty. I put my arms around her and we both cried. "Please forgive me for being such an idiot," I blubbered. "I know it was wrong for me to try to tell you what to do." Suddenly I realized I could never know what was best for someone else. And sadly for me, I knew that my Christmas plans would not include Edris this year.

As it turned out, this was one of my best Christmases ever. I found when I got there just how much I had missed home. All my activities, by choice, centered around home and family traditions. I even helped with the Christmas cooking, with the exception of the fruitcakes, which had always been Aunt Howard's territory. Besides, that was always done before Thanksgiving. Aunt Howard had to have plenty of time to pour the wine, or whiskey or whatever was available over the cakes every few days until they were thoroughly soaked, moist and richly perfumed with the alcohol.

My little sister, Emily, was about eleven or twelve at the time. She had a group of girl friends who spent a lot of time together. I still remember them well: Frances, Mena Claire, Patsy, Mary Grace, Leu Frances, Wanda Lynn, Johnnie Ruth; there may have been others. One day right after I got home they were all at our house doing something very juvenile, I'm sure, when I had a bright idea. These girls had all joined the band and were learning to read music; some of them had been playing the piano for several years. What an opportunity for a budding choral director like me to practice my newly acquired skills! They were such bright, talented little girls. I rounded up all the hymnals

I could find and they learned to sing every Christmas carol worth singing, in parts! Not only did they learn to sing them, but their tone quality was beautiful, and they were able to follow my directing admirably. I began to think becoming a music teacher was the right choice for me. My only disappointment was not having an audience to applaud our efforts, except for our family. But the important thing for me was that I found the "Spirit of Christmas" in the beautiful old carols and the sound of the children's voices, the reflection of the candlelight in their eyes and on their faces. Yes, and the wonder of being able to help bring it to life. How could I hold onto this "Christmas moment?" And then the "Epiphany moment" came as I saw that there would be other Christmases when I would help other children to know the wonder and beauty of Christmas through beautiful music. "Gloria in Excelsis Deo!"

Looking Back 2008 – Music, Music, Music

During my early married years I taught piano lessons and worked with children's choirs. I am thankful today that I had the opportunity to share my love for beautiful music with others, young and old, at school and at church. I spent many happy hours working with children's choirs; for several years my children's choir entertained the local Lions Club members and their wives by singing carols at their Annual Christmas Dinner Party. They looked and sounded like little angels in their white surplices. In later years our family took our children and other family members and friends caroling during the Christmas season. We made our own carol books, and wore jingle bell bracelets and took candles and sang at the homes of neighbors, shut-ins, friends and relatives. One year we had such a large group that we rode in the back of a big U-Haul van, and we'd always come back home afterward for a chili supper. What lovely memories!

Swing Your Partner and Around You Go – NSC Summer of 1947

Did I really pick Edgar Gaddis out of that group of students, standing around the gym floor, waiting for the square dance class to begin? I thought so, but he says it was the other way round; he says he just "knew" I was a good dancer, so he offered to marry me if I would be his dance partner and get him an "A" in the class.

We have each told our own version of that story many times when asked how we met. It has been more than 70 years since that incident occurred; I distinctly remember that it was I who picked *him* out, but I'm not sure why. We did both make an "A" in Social and Square Dance class, which met for eight weeks at 6:00 p.m. in the old Women's Gym at NSC during summer term 1947.

We really enjoyed the class, or maybe we just got in the habit of meeting like that; we kept on long after the term ended. We've been married for more than seventy years now and we still go places together, but we haven't square danced in quite a while. The last time I remember square dancing brings back a host of other good memories.

Looking Back – Philmont Scout Ranch Summer of 1961

It was the summer of 1961 that we took our four children with us to New Mexico when Edgar went for training at Philmont Boy Scout Ranch. Our youngest was still a baby and it sounded like an opportunity for a restful kind of family vacation, which proved to be the case. It was also a lot of fun, in spite of the fact we had to sleep in tents. Everyone ate in a huge, attractive dining hall, and the food was delicious, including my first taste of buffalo, which was super-tasty roast beef to me. While my children were engaged in various age-level activities I was able to participate in sight-seeing trips provided for the wives. At night, after dinner, all of the campers joined in family-style social activities which included movies and yes, square dancing. Then, once the children were settled in bed, the adults had an opportunity to socialize in smaller groups, with other campers from all over the country, in the utility buildings, over coffee and snacks and interesting conversations. That was one of the most relaxing family vacations—about two weeks—that our family ever had. After our stay at Philmont Ranch we continued on to Wyoming, where we visited friends we had made while living there during our first year of marriage.

Edgar and I have maintained our relationship with our Alma Mater NSC (now Northwestern State University) where we first learned to square dance. After graduating there in the summer of 1949, we both went back from time to time and took graduate level courses, and I finally went back and got my MA in Education after my children were in school.

One year after I began teaching, my children and I all spent a summer there together. We lived on campus and took that opportunity to have our wood floors at home refinished. Our oldest son who had finished 9th Grade, enjoyed playing on a baseball team and auditing a freshman math class until I found out he was posing as a college freshman so that he could date college girls. The children and I enjoyed living on campus and eating in the college cafeteria. It was nice for me, not having to cook and keep house for two months and the luxury of being able to attend classes and do research for my Masters' Thesis without having to drive back and forth to Coushatta.

Three of our children later earned their Bachelor's Degrees at Northwestern and our son, Bob, worked there as Comptroller and taught classes at the university for several years. His daughter Amanda played violin in the University Symphony Orchestra and earned her BA Degree in the University's Scholar's College. Edgar and I have enjoyed attending concerts, plays, and many different athletic events at the university throughout the years since we graduated, as well as various kind of alumni events. We still love Northwestern and cherish the years we spent there, and the wonderful people we met during our college years and later in the wider community.

Who's that Man with the Gun? NSC Fall 1947

What a night this has been, I'm thinking to myself, as I look at my watch. What a day and a night. I just hope Shakespeare was right when he said, "All's Well That Ends Well." I think that's what he said. Or was it someone else? And I hope it's gonna end well. Everything seems to be going alright at this point. I hear nothing from the back seat but a little light snoring. Everybody in the car besides me seems to be asleep. No, that's not right. Everybody but the driver and me. I sure hope Edgar will stay awake; he seems to be doing fine so far, but the last time I looked at my watch it seemed to be saying 3:45, and that's a.m. By my calculations we still have another hour or more before we'll be at my home in Coushatta.

Sometimes I do the craziest things. What in the world made me think I could get away with making two dates for the same night, and keeping both of them? When George asked me for a date for this football game, why didn't I just say "no."? But it sounded like fun, so of course, being me, I said "Yes." It would have been so easy to make some kind of excuse at that point, but I never seem to look far enough ahead.

We were out riding that night with the usual bunch and ended up down on the levee eating hot tamales from " Mama Vee's," and George just asked me in a casual kind of way, "how'd you like to go with me and this bunch down to Alexandria for the Northwestern vs. La. College game?" That was over two weeks away, so I just said, almost without thinking, "Oh, gosh, yeah. That sounds like a lotta fun. I haven't made any plans, so count me in. Thanks."

"Oh, it's gonna be fun, alright," George said. "I don't know how good the game will be, but win or lose, it's gonna be a great party. We guys reserved a room at the Bentley Hotel, so we'll have a place to party; before and after the game. How's that sound?"

"Oh—uh. Yeah. That sounds great. Yeah, uh, just great," I agreed. And that's when I began to slow down enough to realize that I had just gotten myself into a complicated situation; in fact I began to wonder how to back out of it without hurting anyone's feelings. There were three other couples and George and me; we'd only dated a few times, mostly very casual stuff, like this little tamale feast on the levee. I was not romantically interested in George, in spite of the fact that he's considered to be one of the best-looking guys on campus. But I was excited about going to the game. I had something new to wear, and I felt real grown-up and sophisticated now that things were beginning to fall into place.

When George explained the details of the plan to me later I began to get cold feet about the whole thing; the big plan was innocent enough; a group party, with those three other couples. The boys pooled their money and got a room at the Bentley Hotel in Alexandria so we would have a place to party before the game and then we could just hang around there after the game until time to go back to the dorm the next day. The problem of course was in the details. Everything would have to fall into place just right for the girls to avoid getting in trouble. For one thing, I would have to sign out for home, which meant I'd have to let Momnee know about the plan, and get her to write me a letter addressed to the Dean of Women giving permission for me to leave campus for the week-end. She might even say "no." It would be humiliating at this point to have to say, "Sorry, gang, I can't make it after all; my mama won't let me go to that kind of party."

In the meantime, the whole plan is getting more convoluted day by day, because it turns out that my sister, Alexa, and my roommate, Marynm Shaw, and their dates, need to spend the rest of the week-end at our house in Coushatta. And Edgar, in whom I do have a romantic interest, finally asks me for a date. The whole thing is getting so problematic that I'm beginning to think I might have to create some kind of "emergency" and just hide out somewhere alone for the week-end. But how in the world could I explain my sudden disappearance and where in the world could I go? No, I'll just have to make it all work somehow.

After a couple of anxious days and sleepless nights, which I deserved because of my own stupidity for getting into such a mess, as it turned out, part of the problem sort of "self-corrected." Maybe fate was on my side after all. Edgar was not just being a jerk waiting so long to ask me for that date; he didn't have a way to go to the game. Edgar, like about 90% of the students at Northwestern now, has no automobile. Only students who live at home in Natchitoches with their families (like George) and a few returning veterans have their own cars. So this is the way it all finally worked out:

Alexa, and Marynm are dating football players, one of whom is a friend of Edgar's, a vet, and has a car. He arranged for Edgar to drive Alexa and Marynm to Alexandria for the game. After the game, the five of them picked me up at the Bentley, where I left George and his bunch to party the rest of the night away and now my new group and I are on our way to Coushatta, where the three of us girls are going to stay for the rest of the week-end. I went with George to the game, as originally planned, but with one small change: I simply explained to George that my mother insisted that I return home with my sister and her date. That was a little embarrassing for me but it seemed to suit George just fine; in retrospect, I'm guessing that he's probably not all that much romantically interested in me either.

The trip home has been uneventful, and now that we're almost home I'm thankful that everything has worked out so well. We did stop at the Blue Moon in Bunkie, kind of a low-class bar with a dance floor, for a restroom break and a few dances. I think it's "off limits" to Northwestern State students, but probably much less risky for me than an all-night party at the grand old historic Bentley hotel in Alexandria would have been. We're almost home now. Edgar is doing the driving, because the other two guys are tired from playing football. The car radio is playing softly and I'm enjoying the music; it's making me sleepy, but we're almost there.

Suddenly, I realize that the car has stopped and Edgar is shaking me gently and whispering, "Wake up, sleepyhead!" I hear sounds of life in the back seat and then with a shock of recognition, I see the familiar outline of my old home on Carroll Street in the little town of Coushatta emerge slowly out of the early morning shadows. I force myself out of my half-awake stupor just in time to see the outline of a man walking at a confident pace down the sidewalk toward our car. Before I can react, Edgar gasps, "Who's that man with the gun?" I can only freeze in disbelief. What on earth is going on?

By this time the whole back seat is in an uproar of confusion, but I am wide awake now and can see in the first rays of morning that the mystery man is my daddy, Bob Stothart. As he puts down his gun and stares at us in confusion, we soon find out that Shakespeare was right; all really is well that ends well. I breathe an audible sigh of relief when we discover that my dad was very innocently waiting on the front porch for his hunting buddy, Oscar Ogilvie to drive up in his car so they can go on an early morning squirrel hunting safari. When Daddy grabs his gun and walks instead toward a car full of trembling college students, our imaginations run wild, of course. There's a moment of comic relief for all of us as we learn that our fears are groundless, but to be perfectly honest, I had to admit to myself that if my daddy had known the whole truth about this escapade of mine, I could have suffered some very embarrassing moments that would not have involved a gun, but would have been far from painless. I have witnessed on many occasions how my daddy is capable of cutting you down to size with a tongue-lashing not soon to be forgotten. I was more than glad that he was able to appreciate the humor in this situation on that long-ago night.

2002 Looking Back

I have laughed to myself many times in later life as I remembered that night when my dad met my future husband, Edgar Gaddis. After we married, the two of them had a long and congenial relationship. Edgar worked for Dad for a while and later bought the business and ran it for years. We even lived with my family for some time, while our own home was being built. They fished and played cards together. But I can remember on several occasions my daddy shaking his head and mumbling clearly enough to be heard easily, "Son-in-laws are mighty poor property."

CHAPTER 11

Life in Cheyenne, 1949-1950

IT IS MID-SEPTEMBER and Edgar and I are now living our dream of adventure in the "Wild West." It is early evening, almost dark, and we are driving in downtown Cheyenne, Wyoming looking for a place to park, when suddenly a light snow begins to fall. Being from the deep south, we're not expecting this; I've never seen snow in September, and it almost seems like a miracle sent from heaven just to welcome us to our new home. We both begin to laugh as the snow starts coming down faster and thicker; huge puffy flakes that whirl faster and faster in the beam of our headlights as the wind begins to pick up. September, and we are in the midst of a "winter wonderland!" Fantastic!

I will always remember that evening because of the snow, but I have no recollection of the reason for our errand in downtown Cheyenne at that time of night. We were just beginning to settle into our apartment, which didn't take long, because at that point in our married life we had collected very few belongings. We had with us only what we could bring on the plane; our clothes and a few other personal belongings. We didn't need much for the two of us in a furnished basement apartment; but that would soon change. We were expecting our first child in late January, and to us in our youthful optimism that was still in the distant future, sometime after we settled into our new situation, Edgar's new job, our first Thanksgiving and Christmas together. All those experiences, in due time would take care of themselves. We had no suspicion that the basement apartment we had just moved into would be only one of three that we would live in during our short year's sojourn in Cheyenne.

While Edgar was adjusting to his new job as assistant coach and Math teacher to Jr. High School students, I began adjusting to caring for two little girls, to help pay our rent. Those little girls, Marilyn Kaye, a preschooler, and Jody, who was in kindergarten, lived upstairs with

Our first home in Cheyenne

their mother, a divorcee and librarian who owned this house and basement apartment we were living in. I would be responsible for the care of the two little girls during their after-school hours and for providing their evening meals, in exchange for reduced rent payments.

Their mother gave me only a very sketchy informal job description with no specific instructions or rules, but she was careful to warn me forcefully that both girls were severely allergic to peaches and tomatoes. I assured her equally as emphatically that I understood the seriousness of allergies and would be constantly on guard to ensure that her little girls would never come in contact with those two enemies on my watch.

When I explained the situation to Edgar, (we both loved peaches) we were able to give them up without too much grief. Tomatoes, however, proved to be more of a challenge. I fumed and struggled and finally with much regret put tomatoes on the prohibited list when shopping for groceries. The biggest problem with that was that in spite of the rent reduction we received, we were living on a very restricted (beginning teacher's) income and the recipes for most of the low-budget dishes that I knew how to cook listed tomatoes as one of the essential ingredients. (Think spaghetti sauce and vegetable soup.) It was quite a challenge but I did manage to keep my word to our librarian landlady. In fact, she actually complimented me on what nice, well-balanced meals I served her children. However, learning to cook and eat without tomatoes did not solve all my child-care woes.

Sometime in early November the two little girls managed to get their mouths around a spoonful or more of either peaches or tomatoes, or both, somewhere outside my household. They both broke out in the worst case of hives you could ever hope to see. The poor little things were covered with a horrible red rash from heads-to-toes; could barely open their eyes. It was a pitiful thing to see. I spent my days reading stories, singing songs to them, giving them their medicine, anything to distract them from their woes (no TV available in those ancient times.) Then when and if there was time, I prayed for their healing and my sanity.

Toward the end of a dreadful week of these horrendous afflictions the doorbell rang upstairs one day and I opened the door to a tall, pleasant-looking man, who asked to see his little daughters. I was in shock when I realized who he was, and having had no prior warning that this situation might occur, I let him in, and did my best to explain the little girls' condition, trying meanwhile to answer his questions without making matters worse. He was obviously upset, and looking for someone to blame, but somehow we got through a very awkward meeting without it becoming a serious incident.

A totally different incident, however, soon led to our being asked by Mrs. Landlady-librarian to find other living arrangements; unlike the allergy episode, it *was* my fault. She had every right to be angry, I took responsibility for it then, and can find no valid excuse for my irresponsibility. I'm just glad that nothing tragic happened as a result of my youthful carelessness. At the time we rented that apartment I was young, but old enough to understand that I was accepting full responsibility for the care of those two young children. Their mother told me that it was okay to leave them taking their naps upstairs as long as I brought them downstairs with me as soon as they woke. One day I went to sleep reading a book, and they were on their own without any supervision for long enough to open the front door to the mailman and receive a package which turned out to be toys intended to go under the Christmas tree. By the time I awoke the damage was done. They had managed to tear into the package, discover the surprises within—much too soon—and leave a wide array of evidence scattered about the premises.

I was ashamed; in fact, devastated that I had been so unreliable in my duties, and I hope that in remembering this incident I grew to be a more careful, more responsible person, in large matters and small. I did not purposefully neglect my duties, but my lack of awareness in this situation could have caused serious damage, regardless of my intentions. I also knew that our finding another apartment was not going to be easy, but in the end, I did learn a lesson from this mistake. It helped me to realize that being a responsible person is worth the effort.

Finding another furnished basement apartment where children were permitted was not easy, but the search was worth the time and effort. We found one that was not only attractive and comfortable, but of all things, it had a piano. That basement had once been the setting for a large kitchen-guest-room and recreation-room, (that explained the piano) but it also had a fireplace with a gas heater in it and pine paneling on the walls. Better still—it was owned by an elderly Greek widow, Mrs. Fotopolis, and her young, unmarried daughter, who were the nicest,

friendliest people you
could ever hope to
meet, and—best of all,
they loved children,
and were excited to find
that we were expect-
ing a baby in January.
I could hardly believe
our good luck.

Our home with Mrs. Fotopolis

Not only was Mrs. Fotopolis a friendly and motherly
person, she was also a marvelous cook. As the holiday
season approached she brought delicious home-made
Greek pastries such as baklava down to the basement for
us to enjoy. This was my first time to taste such delicacies,
and to me they were better than any other baked product
I had ever eaten. Years later, after we came back home to
Louisiana I was delighted to see ads in the Shreveport
newspapers at Thanksgiving and Christmas by Greek
Orthodox Churches offering them for sale at fund-raisers.
I would race that 50 miles to buy them before they were
all gone. Every bite I ate of those delicious little pastries
reminded me of Mrs. Fotopolis and the happy months
we spent in her basement immediately prior to and after
the birth of our first child.

When I received a letter from my sister, Alexa, who was
in school at Northwestern State College informing me
that she and John Osborne were planning to be married
during the Christmas Holidays, my first reaction was
disappointment; I, of course, would not be able to attend
the wedding. However, I soon received a phone call from
her saying that they were thinking about coming out

west for their wedding trip, and I was overjoyed when they accepted our invitation to spend a few days with us during their trip.

Alexa and I had been almost inseparable as children. We were just 18 months apart in age, and shared a bedroom through childhood and youth right up until I left to go to college at Northwestern. We stayed close at NSC, but had gradually begun to lead separate lives by the time I graduated; still, we missed each other. I was happy to be with her again for those few short days at Christmas time, and to do some fun things together and get to know her new husband a little better. On Christmas Eve we drove to Laramie to the Little Remount Inn, at the Remount Ranch, the home of Mary O'Hara, author of *My Friend, Flicka* and other best-selling novels about Wyoming. It was a picturesque setting for a festive Christmas Eve dinner. There was no snow falling that evening but plenty on the ground; a lovely Christmas card scene.

The next day we had Christmas dinner at noon in Cheyenne with Edgar's oldest brother, Gene and his family at their home. Gene's wife, Anita (Neet) had cooked a delicious traditional turkey dinner, which was a wonderful and homey way for all of us to celebrate Christmas with family far from home. There were three generations at the dinner table; Gene and Neet's oldest two children, Ken and Kathy were about eight and five years old, the three couples were the middle generation, and Neet's elderly mother, Mrs. Beismeier, who was living with them, was the only grandparent present. The children were on their best behavior, (they always were) and seemed to enjoy being in the company of all these adult relatives; it was a delightful family holiday gathering with good food and loving fellowship.

Not long after Christmas I had a frightening experience; a gas leak in our fireplace heater. I had nothing important to do so I decided to pamper myself and sleep a little longer than usual. It was a very cold morning and I wouldn't have the choice to sleep in much longer. My baby was due in less than a month. As a matter of fact, I almost slept through the rest of my life; by the time my sister-in-law, Neet got me to the hospital my doctor was unable to find any fetal heart tones. Through a lucky accident, (a miracle is what I called it), baby and I survived, and about two weeks later, on January 12, 1950 I gave birth to a healthy baby boy, Robert Eugene Gaddis, at Laramie County Memorial Hospital. When we got home from the hospital Edgar stayed home with us for a few days, and then my mother came and stayed about a week to get us off to a good start.

I had no experience in caring for an infant, but I felt more confident after Momnee came and spent a little time with us. Just knowing that Mrs. Fotopolis was upstairs made me feel much more secure, too. By the end of February things were beginning to seem almost normal again. Baby Bob was thriving and Edgar and I were surviving, and learning how to handle all the difficult things they don't warn you about in all the "how-to" books. There were some surprises; I found out right away that a clothes drier is almost unnecessary in Wyoming. It is so dry and cold and windy that by the time I'd hung out one clothesline full of diapers the first ones had already frozen dry. That's convenient, but not really a very comfortable way to get the job done.

Now it's March and I'm feeling like everything is beginning to fall into place for us. We had a visit from the Welcome Wagon with all kinds of goodies for us and the baby, and I accepted an invitation to attend the Newcomers' Club. It was a potluck supper and I took fried chicken as my contribution, which was a smashing success. It was the first time I had actually made fried chicken all by myself, but I'd watched Aunt Howard make it about a million times. Everyone declared it was the best they'd ever eaten, and I'm sure that was because it was the first time they had ever eaten real "Southern Fried Chicken."

We are now members of First Methodist Church in Cheyenne. Edgar's family are mostly Baptist, I think, but he wasn't really happy in the Baptist Church. He wasn't much of a churchgoer when I met him, but church has always been a big part of my life. When we talked about it he explained that he never did feel called to go down to the altar and confess that he had been saved. Now he has decided to join the Methodist Church here with me, and I'm glad. I want to bring my children up in church, and I'd rather it would be the Methodist Church, since I was a member of Wesley Foundation while I was at Northwestern, went to First Methodist in Natchitoches and sang in the Chancel Choir there the whole time I was in college. I just feel more at home in the Methodist Church and with Methodist beliefs and teachings.

Life is good. I'm beginning to feel more at home here

Evelyn and Dick Enzian, Edgar, Joy and baby Bob

in Cheyenne. We have two couples now that we can call friends. The Rectors, Bill and Norma, know us because of the school connection. Bill is football coach at the Junior High, and Edgar is his assistant. We met Dick and Evelyn Enzian through Gene and Neet. Dick is in the Air Force, stationed at Fort Warren Air Force Base where Edgar's brother, Gene works. We see the Rectors mostly at school events, and we enjoy playing cards and just visiting with the Enzians. They are about our age and have no children yet. I am really beginning to feel like a part of Edgar's family now that we have become so connected to Gene and his family. I like living in this apartment much better than the first one. It has its disadvantages; (we have to go through the furnace room to get to the kitchen,) but for the first time now I feel that we can invite friends over, and we're beginning to feel like a part of the community.

As the school year progresses Edgar seems to enjoy his work and I am beginning to love my new life, and "family" and home.

Well! Life can be strange; complicated, and full of surprises! Just as I am beginning to feel a sense of belonging here in this new place, along comes a big Greek wedding and turns everything upside down. I think I am beginning to understand the meaning of the word irony. We came here in the first place as a sort of adventure, wanting to see what it would be like to live in a very different kind of place; wondering whether or not we would want to stay. Then just as we begin to feel like it's what we want to do, and that we can actually do it, the bottom falls out. Here's what happened:

Mrs. Fotopolis couldn't bring herself to tell us, so without any warning one day she sent her daughter downstairs to break the news that she (the daughter) is getting married. She is having a big church wedding; a big Greek church wedding; with all the relatives coming from Greece, and staying for weeks; and all that big family needing to be together for the festivities; at this house and in this nice apartment we have just begun to love and think of as our home.

Oh, well! This time the apartment search should be a little easier; we only need to find a place to stay for a couple of months. It should be as close to the school as possible, decent enough to live in, but cheap. We don't have to like the place; we can stand almost anything for a couple of months. School will be out in June and then we can pack our bags again and head for Louisiana for another hot summer. We'll have a whole summer to decide whether or not we want to come back. My family has a big house and would love having us—and their first grandchild—with them for the summer, while we decide on our permanent plans.

In the meantime we found just the kind of apartment we were looking for: near the school, decent, cheap. It was as bad as we had expected; in an industrial area near the school, small, but clean. It was furnished, but the furnishings were minimal; a one-room house with a former life as a garage. It was a slightly elongated box with a bed on one end and a huge coal range that cooked the meals, heated the place, and heated the water for the bathroom on the other end. Yes, it did have a bathroom with a tub that was six feet long, and a coal shed that was a little too far from the house for my comfort. I soon found out that April and May are WINTER months in Wyoming.

During those last two months in Cheyenne I lived the simple life: Shoveled coal and stoked the fire, cared for our baby, cooked our meals, shoveled coal and stoked the fire, cleaned the house and cared for the baby, shoveled coal. While Edgar taught school, coached, shoveled coal – oh well, I'm sure by now you've got the picture. (I'd never built a coal fire before, and never quite learned how.)

One morning in mid-April Edgar reminded me as he left for a day of teaching at Johnson Junior High School that he would be later than usual getting home because he had to go after school with the team to a track meet in Greeley, Colorado, which was about 50 miles from Cheyenne. He also reminded me not to dare let the fire go out. I hadn't yet learned how to get it going again when that happened, and the weather was supposed to get colder.

The simple life just got more challenging. I brought in coal and kept that fire going all day, but when night came I began to wonder how late Edgar might be coming home. It had been snowing all day long in Cheyenne, so the weather couldn't be much better in Greeley. When it got to be about ten o'clock I began to worry. Finally I decided to take Bob out of his crib and put him in bed with me so I could keep him warm in case the fire went out. When Edgar finally got home sometime between one and two o'clock in the morning he found the two of us asleep in a too-cozy-warm room with the wall behind the stove beginning to give off a soft red glow. The snowstorm delayed him, but he got home just in time to prevent the fire.

The month of May started out a little warmer, so we tried planning a picnic with Dick and Evelyn Enzian for Memorial Day, but unfortunately it had to be held indoors because of a late snow storm, so we soon began making our plans for our trip back home to Louisiana. (I'm feeling a little homesick just thinking about it.) We left home in the spirit of adventure, but our dream didn't exactly include a long, long winter like this one has been, and according to the natives this was no winter at all compared to the one last year.

When Edgar and I began loading our belongings into the car early on the morning of June 3, 1950 to come home to Louisiana for the summer, a light snow began falling and by the time we were pulling out of the drive-way of our little one-room house on the wrong side of the railroad tracks, there was a thin layer of snow on the top and hood of our car. I couldn't help thinking maybe this time the snow is saying, "Good-bye."

CHAPTER 12

Elm Grove Plantation

Back Home in Louisiana

SUMMERTIME, 1950, and "the livin' was easy" especially for Baby Bob and me. We were back in my hometown of Coushatta, spending the summer with my parents, until time for Edgar to resume his job teaching Math to eight and ninth graders in Cheyenne, Wyoming in the Fall. We spent a little time visiting his parents and his brothers and their families who lived in various parts of the state. It was fun for me, getting to know his brothers and their families better and showing off our new baby to everyone. He was quite an attraction in my parents' home, where he was the first and only grandchild. When we visited relatives on Edgar's side of the family he had to share the spotlight with a few other grandchildren and cousins, but there was enough attention to go around. It was a good summer.

However, it was not quite so easy for Edgar; being of sound mind and full of youthful energy, he soon tired of all the adulation and conversation that go with

Painting the Big House

getting re-acquainted with relatives and old friends. He found himself a job repainting my parents' large old Victorian-era home. This proved to be a more challenging task than he had expected, but he managed to stick with it by limiting his working time (mostly) to the coolest hours of the day, which became fewer and shorter as June turned into July. It was a typical scorching Louisiana summer, but in spite of that when Edgar's brother Joe approached him about the possibility of a more permanent job nearby, we didn't have to struggle long over the decision. Our original excitement at experiencing an adventure in the "wild west" was beginning to pale in comparison with the comfort and joy that we were feeling now as we allowed ourselves to anticipate the possibility of returning to live in the familiar surroundings of family and the relaxed southern lifestyle we had left behind.

Edgar's brother, Joe had graduated from the University of Arkansas with a degree in Agri-business, and was working as overseer for the Elm Grove Plantation near Shreveport, Louisiana. When Joe learned that the plantation owners needed someone to manage the plantation commissary he passed that information on to Edgar; we talked about it briefly, he applied for the job and was hired. Joe and his wife, Jerry and their two small children, Jeff and Linda who were just a little older than our own baby, were living in one of the plantation-owned houses. Joe had been working there several years and had found the Hodges family, the owners, to be good people to work for. We decided to exchange a "home on the range" for a small house on a southern plantation with no rent or utilities to pay, and a modest but acceptable salary.

By the time we moved into our little cottage, which belonged to the plantation and was within easy walking distance of the Commissary, we had painted the living room and kitchen in colors that harmonized with our hand-me-down furniture, discarded from the homes of our parents and other relatives. We finally had a place to put to use the wedding gifts we had to leave behind when we went to Wyoming. Elm Grove, a tiny community, a wide spot in the road really, with a beautiful little Baptist church, plantation store, a little settlement of cabins for the field hands, and some larger, handsomer dwellings belonging to the plantation owners; yes, Elm Grove, Louisiana and it's become home to Edgar and me and our son, Bob.

Life on Elm Grove Plantation

Today is August 28,1951 and it's hard to believe that Bob is 18 months old now. Sometimes it's just hard to realize that I am a mom. Most of the time I am so involved in being one that I don't even have time to think about it. He's "cute as a bug" and every bit as active. He has a pet rabbit which he calls "Nunny Daddit" that lives on our screened porch, and I encourage him to spend a lot of his time playing out there too.

Located on Louisiana Highway 71, and just two houses north of the plantation commissary (known as W.H. & C.B. Hodges Store), is the small, somewhat rickety, but not quite dilapidated, white frame house we call home. Joe and Jerry live about a half mile from us in a larger and considerably nicer house than the one we live in. It's good having family so close to us.

Our two families share a milk cow. I don't know where we got her. (Probably on loan from the plantation.) Edgar milks in the morning and Joe at night and we share the milk and the cost of feed for the cow. I never thought my mother's sage advice from her grandmother, "never learn to milk a cow," would come in handy for me, but when this cow-sharing experience began I thanked the Good Lord that Momnee had the presence of mind to pass this bit of wisdom along. Otherwise, who knows? I might still be milking a cow when I'm old and gray. And here's another scary thought. What if I happened to actually enjoy milking? Then when it was my turn to hand out advice, I might encourage my own daughter, if I have one, to learn to milk. Think of the implications: It could get to be a family tradition, which in itself might not be a bad thing, but when you consider all the possibilities (one of Edgar's brothers ended up owning a dairy) well, let's just say the situation could get seriously out of control. My great-grandmother said it. My mother said it. Now I am saying it; are you listening? "Don't ever learn to milk a cow."

All things considered we have a pretty good life here in Elm Grove; very little money but plenty of milk, cream for our cornflakes, homemade ice cream, butter and cottage cheese. We have a garden, half a cow and our neighbors seem like good folks. The Guillorys next door often send their eleven-year-old twins, Mabel and Sable over to look after Bob for a little while so I can have a break. In a sort of implicit exchange I then ask the girls to stay for supper, which they've never yet declined to do. They tell me how to make real good Cajun foods like gumbo and other foods that start with a roux, and they eat great quantities of whatever foods I set before them. They're cute kids, and well-behaved. I'm enjoying learning more about the Cajun culture. I don't know what brought that family to this part of the state, but I'm glad they came.

Irene Gay who is our neighbor on the other side gives me lots of free advice on child rearing, especially toilet-training, which according to her is way overdue for eighteen-month-old Bob, "especially with a new baby on the way; think of all those diapers!" She hounds me at least once a day; oftener when the occasion demands. I have to admit, she has a point; after all, I am still washing with a "rub board" until we can afford a washing machine. I'm holding off on the toilet training for the time being, however. I have to give Dr. Benjamin Spock's advice precedence over my neighbor's, even though she does have a six-year-old. Doctor Spock and I won the first battle but I'm afraid the war's not over yet.

We're having a real Louisiana summer; record high temperatures; no relief in sight. I'm having some morning sickness now. The window fan in the bedroom doesn't help much. My solution to the situation is to take my laundry once or twice a week to my parents' home in Coushatta, which *does* help considerably. Not only do Edgar and I *not* own a washing machine, now we don't even have decent water. The small inconvenience of driving 28 miles to Coushatta is more than offset by the availability of modern laundry equipment, good water and the comfort of a relatively cool house. There are always family members available and eager to take Bob off my hands for a little while so I can visit and relax.

Edgar doesn't even miss us on our laundry days because his hours at the store are long. He seems to enjoy his work, in spite of the long, hot days. It is quite a change from teaching math to eighth-graders. It seems a shame, in a way, because he really does have a talent for teaching, and I know it was a great disappointment for his dad, but teaching just wasn't for him; or rather, the $179 a month just wasn't enough for the three of us.

The plantation store, or "commissary," as they call it, is quite an interesting place, Edgar says. He has learned a lot about the old plantation system, and according to him, nothing has really changed much since slavery days. The store seems to be right at the center of plantation life. The plantation offices are located in the back of the store and sometimes owners of neighboring plantations will come by to talk, and drink a coke. Edgar has begun making and selling sandwiches for people who come by at noon; there are gas pumps out front, so people in the area come by to fill up their vehicles and catch up on the news. It's a sociable place.

Edgar has one part-time helper, a black man whom everyone calls "Piece o'Man" because one side of his body is paralyzed (from a stroke I suppose.) Edgar says that is all the help he needs. The store work is not all that hard, but the hours are long. Most of his customers are the farm (field) hands, who have free housing and gas from the plantation wells and water from the cisterns; they are transported to the fields each day in the back of trucks belonging to the plantation by drivers who are employed by the plantation. Sounds like a pretty good deal, doesn't it?

But here's how the system actually works: The hands work for a daily wage, that is handed to them once every two weeks in the form of "scrip," which is simply a piece of paper stating that the bearer is entitled to goods from the commissary equal to a stated sum of money. It is not good for cash except in unusual circumstances, and exceptions are frowned upon. The laborers are dependent on the commissary for all their material goods, except for items such as shoes, which the commissary doesn't

"Piece o'Man" and Edgar at Elm Grove Plantation Commissary

carry. They are allowed to buy on credit up to a certain amount, and most of them stay in debt and can probably vouch for the truth in the familiar words of a "Tennessee Ernie" song, " . . . I owe my soul to the company store."

Sometimes, when there are disagreements between tenant laborers and the owners, the tenants will surreptitiously approach a neighboring plantation owner, asking to be "hired on," with all that entails, for the next year. If the owner agrees, he then approaches the present employer and offers an amount negotiated and agreed upon between the two, and the laborer now "belongs to him," and in a sense is his responsibility. Owners' responsibilities to tenants are not usually stated, but can include such varied services as getting needed medical attention and using their influence, or money, to get the workers out of jail when necessary, and from what I hear this happens fairly often.

The water system here is primitive. We have a big cistern which I'm looking at now from the kitchen window. The rain falls into it and that's how God provides our drinking water, and water for washing and everything else. What I mean by that is, it's free just like the house rent, which is fine with me until it stops raining for a while. You know the old saying, "You get just about what you pay for." Well, after the first month of no rain the water turns sort of dense-looking. It seems to me there are definitely things in that liquid that shouldn't be drunk, even when it's turned into coffee. And then, sometimes the unthinkable happens; no water at all. Another old saying: "You don't miss the water 'til the well (or cistern) runs dry" which happened to us, recently.

The next thing I know, a big truck with a tank on back pulls up and begins pumping something into the cistern. I find myself looking out the window, eye-to-eye with someone who looks like he could be Piece o' Man's brother, or at least his first cousin. He must have interpreted the question on my face as disapproval, I think that because the first words out of his mouth are, "Oh, don't worry none, Ma'am, I's jest bringin' y'alls wawtuh fo' the house. Hope y'all ain't been out long, Ma'am, but we jes' hadda haul dat cotton piz'n to the hanguh 'fo' I cud git ovuh heah with the wawtuh. Airplane's gotta dus' 'at cotton, y' know; we don't make no cotton, don't nobody eat."

Well, for days after that happens, every time I turn on the water faucet I imagine I can smell cotton poison. I keep telling myself my imagination is just working overtime . . . or is it? SURELY they wouldn't haul our water in the same tank they hauled cotton poison in . . . or would they? It's no comfort at all to remind myself of the little witticism Edgar uses with our neighbor who is a crop duster and *always* smells of cotton poison: "Oh, well, you'll never be bothered with mosquito bites again."

November 19, 1951 – Life on the Ol'
Plantation

Thank goodness it has finally turned a little cooler here; August was such a scorcher. Fall here is very different from what we experienced in Wyoming, and the nice cool temperatures have reaffirmed my feelings that we were right to come back home to the South. There's not much going on here at our house, except that Bob is growing so *fast*. He's talking a lot now, and looking forward to the new baby.

I looked out the kitchen window the other day, and almost gasped in amazement as I saw Bob's little face looking right back at me from a ladder, about six feet off the ground. I ran as fast as I could in my expectant condition, to try to apprehend him before he realized he was up so high. He has *never* climbed before; always seemed a bit afraid of heights. Thank goodness I made it in time, but I knew immediately that my troubles were not over. Now that he realizes he can do it, he *likes* climbing; I just hope he doesn't start climbing out of his crib before we can get him a regular kiddy bed.

We don't have much spare time, but when we do have a little time to relax, Bob and I can spend it now by watching Edgar play softball. He plays in a Shreveport League with some of his old college buddies. We also share these amusements with a couple I went to high school with, Jack and Billie Holley. Jack plays on the team as well, and Billie and I take Bob and their little girl Sherry, who is almost three, and watch the games together. Edgar and Jack also make a little extra cash by refereeing high school basketball games. Sometimes Billie and I take the kids and go along to these games as well. That isn't quite as pleasant, however, because the rivalries between these little rural schools can get fierce, just short of violence. Some of the fans (especially parents) get pretty fired up when things aren't going well for their team, which of course is always the fault of the referees. They even adopt a threatening attitude, and yell ugly things. On one such occasion a loud voice bellowed from directly behind Billie and me, "The referee's a Jackass!"

On Sundays we go to the little Baptist Church here. We attend Sunday School and I play the piano for services when a substitute is needed for the regular pianist. It's a beautiful little church, built and funded primarily, I understand, by the families of two sweet old ladies, Miss Mary Hodges and "Miss" Virginia Mercer. They are sisters and part owners in the plantation here. Miss Mary invited me to come and practice the piano at her house, since we don't have one. (Yet.) Maybe my playing is worse than I thought! Actually they have both been very sweet and welcoming to me, and have had Bob and me over to visit. I think they are pleased that Edgar and I have chosen to attend their church rather than drive to the nearest Methodist Church in Bossier.

February 9, 1952 – Welcome to the Newborn!

I'm writing from my bed at Schumpert Hospital in Shreveport to record the arrival of our beautiful baby girl, Ellen Howard Gaddis, on February 6. We are both doing well and expect to go home to Elm Grove tomorrow or the next day. Edgar's mother, "Miss" Effie, will be coming to our house to spend the first week with her new granddaughter. She is absolutely the world's greatest mother-in-law; never interfering, but always glad to help when needed. (The nurse just brought Ellen in for her breast-feeding, and she sounds hungry, so I'll finish writing this later.)

We're home now with the new baby, and both children

are sleeping. Miss Effie has been wonderful help with the kids and won't let me do a thing but nurse Ellen, who is a very good baby; no colic, or other problems so far. She seems to be happy with the way we and the rest of the world are treating her, so far. Bob is a different story.

Apparently he forgot to tell us he wanted to remain an only child. The first hint we had of this was when Ellen began to cry the other night and he suggested we put her in the garbage can. Then when he came in the bedroom yesterday morning and found me in the rocking chair, nursing her, he brought a story book and tried to climb up in my lap with her. When I tried to explain to him that I would read it later, he began wailing and crying, "now, Now, NOW!" We finally got the message when, in the middle of the night, he came riding into our bedroom on his new Christmas tricycle, and climbed into bed with us. Poor little fellow; he now knows that his life will never be quite the same.

Ellen and Bob

Bob is learning new tricks every day now. Yesterday he decided to show off one of the newest of these exploits for the benefit of his Grandma as we were having breakfast. As she was pouring orange juice in the glasses he banged that little fist on the highchair tray and cried out, "More beer!" While he didn't get the same rousing cheers in response from good

Baptist Grandma that he always gets from Daddy's friends I could tell that his daddy was proud of him by the way he covered his face with his hands. Bob is also proving to be quite a problem-solver. He was playing outside in his sand box this afternoon when I called him to come in because it was starting to rain. The next thing I knew, he dumped a whole bucket of sand on the kitchen floor and sat down to play.

We will be showing off both children in Coushatta to another set of grandparents and various other relatives this week-end on our way to take Grandma Gaddis home to Pleasant Hill. I'm sure going to miss her next week and for a long time to come. It would be nice if we could keep her with us at least until they're ready to start school.

Looking Back on Spring and Summer 1952

Our life on the plantation was mostly uneventful, which suited us at that time in our lives. We enjoyed visiting with Edgar's brother, Joe and his family and were close enough to Coushatta to visit my parents often. We went to the Elm Grove Baptist Church on Sundays, where I took Bob to Sunday school and joined an adult Sunday School Class. We attended worship services there and I even served as substitute for the pianist when she was absent, which pleased Miss Mary Hodges and her sister, Miss Virginia, two elderly sisters, who were co-owners of the plantation along with their brothers. Their family had been founders of that beautiful little church, and if

I am not mistaken, played a very significant role in the erection of the church building. We enjoyed being "part-time Baptists" there for a while.

While living and working there Edgar somehow found time to play ball, and also to referee ball games in the area with Jack Holley. We became close friends with him and his wife, Billie, and it was a friendship that lasted for many years. We had many enjoyable adventures with this couple, including a trip to Yellowstone Park.

It was the summer after Ellen's birth that I received a phone call from my mother, warning us not to come to visit in Coushatta because they were experiencing a serious and tragic Polio epidemic. There were a large number of families who had children affected and they were all friends and acquaintances of ours. It was a very frightening experience for people in the whole area, and the consequences for many were life-threatening and for some life-changing.

This was, of course, before any preventive drugs had been developed. I will *never* forget how frightening those days were for me as a parent and what a happy day it was when we were finally able to take our children to get the "sugar cube" and later the perfected polio vaccine. I can still remember the days from my own childhood when the opening of school would sometimes have to be postponed, and swimming pools and other recreational areas and public places closed down because of Polio epidemics. I am thankful to God and to Dr. Jonah Salk and others that the terrible disease is no longer a threat to children.

Now if our country can just marshal the will and

the financing to launch an all-out crusade against other life-threatening diseases such as cancer and heart disease, our world will be a much better place. I think it will take the kind of perseverance and sacrifice that our country made during World War II. No one that I knew ever complained about making sacrifices then. We were just taught that it was the right thing to do.

CHAPTER 13

A Home Again

Our Own Little House and How It Grew

IN 1954, WE MOVED into our own little house on Clarkson Street in Coushatta, and began to make it our permanent home. I taught piano part time and also did substitute work in classrooms mostly at Coushatta

Bob Gaddis and Steve Osborne, Clarkson Street, 1954

Bob and Ellen in our Coushatta home, 1954

Elementary School. I started to consider myself a full-time mother and homemaker, although I never again completely left the teaching profession until I finally retired in 1995.

Our family continued to grow as our second daughter, Blanche appeared on the scene of her big sister Ellen's third birthday, February 6, 1955, even though she had to drag around and be sixteen days late to get the date just right. Now our little house was beginning to feel a bit tight in the seams so we added a small utility room and soon completed the expansion upstairs to its full potential of two generous sized bedrooms and a bath.

Some five years later our family reached its maximum size when baby brother Tom arrived on September 19, 1960. I remember drawing the plans for a 2-room expansion downstairs while still in the hospital recuperating from his birth. Thankfully, cousin Wayne Ponder was still in the area building houses, and agreed to do the

Blanche, Ellen, Tom, and Bob

work for us; again, from my rough sketches. In a few months' time we had a new living room and dining room wing on the house, with the old living room turned into a good-sized family room partially open to the kitchen. This worked well for us as the children grew to be teens and then left for college, marriage, careers, and homes and families of their own.

For some reason, though, our little house couldn't stop growing. We just seemed to enjoy spreading out. We gradually began adding living spaces to the outdoors. Patios, porches, terraces; they just seemed to appear everywhere. We might be outdoors working on flower beds and before we knew it, we had pulled up a few chairs so neighbors out for a walk could sit and talk a while, and next thing, it became a screened porch opening into the dining room, or a deck connecting our bedroom and bath to the pool. When we finally added a much-needed carport to the house it just begged for a front porch connecting to the front entrance; one thing led to another, and we added a bay window area that gave us more space in the family room.

The last significant addition to our little house was a screened addition to the living-dining wing that gave us space for an outdoor kitchen-eating area connected to the dining room and indoor kitchen by French- doors that gave us room for big family gatherings with children, grandchildren and great-grandchildren. Our house has always been a work-in-progress; I think our granddaughter, Jane Frederick, described it best when she was explaining to her husband, Adam, the way she pictured our house: "Always there, but never the same".

Our house on Clarkson Street, after it grew

Acknowledgments

I have seldom found myself at a loss for words. But as I allow myself to feel the joy of completing an undertaking that has stretched over a lifetime, I find that I am groping for the right ones now.

God has provided me with the undeserved blessings of guidance and help when I had the wisdom to accept.

My daughters, Ellen Howell and Blanche Hirsch, have worked faithfully and tirelessly on the essential creative tasks of producing a "real book." I am deeply grateful to Ellen for her wonderful illustrations, as well. Thanks to my great-granddaughter Emma Greer, and my son-in-law Matthew Hirsch, for the help with proof-reading.

My many family members and close friends have been supportive encouragers. And my husband, Edgar, has been my best critic and ally throughout.